Assessing Dyslexia

In today's schools, teachers must screen and monitor for academic difficulties and are expected to use assessments to guide their instruction. Understanding the assessment of students with dyslexia gives teachers the knowledge to identify which skills need remediation and the students' strengths that can help them overcome their challenges. *Assessing Dyslexia* provides teachers with answers to questions they often have about assessment and is applicable not only to students with dyslexia but to all who struggle with reading.

Written in accessible terms throughout, this book offers information on understanding and interpreting psychoeducational reports and approaches on how to better communicate with parents and students regarding this process. By demonstrating how to use testing to guide their teaching, this book describes the why, how and what of assessment and promotes the self-sufficiency of teachers by providing them with a clear rationale for why particular instructional strategies should be used.

With encouragement for teachers to reflect on assessment critically and resources to expand their skill knowledge, this book provides a clear path to enhancing teachers' practice and improving their pupils' attainment. *Assessing Dyslexia* serves as a suitable reading for all teachers and represents a move from the "wait to fail" model to a test to teach approach, addressing the questions and anxieties of today's teachers.

Gad Elbeheri is the founder and chairman of Global Educational Consultants, Egypt. He is Director at Large of the International Dyslexia Association (IDA) and Chair of the IDA Global Partners Committee. He is also a member of the Professional Advisory Board of the Learning Disabilities Association of America (LDA).

Eric Q. Tridas is the founder and senior partner of The Tridas Group. He is an International Dyslexia Association (IDA) representative to the National Joint Committee on Learning Disabilities (NJCLD) and a member of the Professional Advisory Board of the Learning Disability Association of America (LDA).

Assessing Dyslexia
A Teacher's Guide to Understanding and Evaluating their Pupils' Needs

Gad Elbeheri and Eric Q. Tridas

Routledge
Taylor & Francis Group
LONDON AND NEW YORK

Cover image: © Getty Images

First published 2023
by Routledge
4 Park Square, Milton Park, Abingdon, Oxon OX14 4RN

and by Routledge
605 Third Avenue, New York, NY 10158

Routledge is an imprint of the Taylor & Francis Group, an informa business

© 2023 Gad Elbeheri and Eric Q. Tridas

The right of Gad Elbeheri and Eric Q. Tridas to be identified as authors of this work has been asserted in accordance with sections 77 and 78 of the Copyright, Designs and Patents Act 1988.

All rights reserved. No part of this book may be reprinted or reproduced or utilised in any form or by any electronic, mechanical, or other means, now known or hereafter invented, including photocopying and recording, or in any information storage or retrieval system, without permission in writing from the publishers.

Trademark notice: Product or corporate names may be trademarks or registered trademarks, and are used only for identification and explanation without intent to infringe.

British Library Cataloguing-in-Publication Data
A catalog record has been requested for this book

ISBN: 978-1-032-07917-2 (hbk)
ISBN: 978-1-032-07915-8 (pbk)
ISBN: 978-1-003-21205-8 (ebk)

DOI: 10.4324/9781003212058

Typeset in Bembo
by Apex CoVantage, LLC

Contents

	Preface	vii
1	The Nature of Dyslexia Assessment	1
	Introduction & Definition	*1*
	Dyslexia: Prevalence & Signs	*3*
	Importance of Dyslexia Assessment	*5*
	Fundamentals of Dyslexia Assessment	*5*
	Types of Dyslexia Assessments	*7*
	Purpose of Dyslexia Assessment	*10*
2	The LEFT Model: A Process for Dyslexia Assessment	12
	Components of Dyslexia Assessment	*12*
	The Rule of Fours	*13*
	The LEFT Model	*15*
	Listen: History	*16*
	Evaluate: Testing and Documentation	*17*
	Formulate: Putting It All Together	*18*
	Teach/Treat	*18*
3	Listen	20
	The Educational History: Developmental Profile and Academic Work	*21*
	Behaviour/Emotional Regulation	*22*
	Health	*23*
	Environment	*24*
4	Evaluate: Teacher Assessment of Language & Literacy	27
	Checklists for Teachers	*28*
	Screening Tools for Teachers	*30*
	Error Analysis	*32*

vi *Contents*

	Progress Monitoring & RTI	*34*
	Behavioural Observations	*35*
5	Evaluate: Understanding a Psychoeducational Evaluation Report	37
	Test Types	*37*
	Interpreting Test Results	*43*
6	Formulation: Putting It All Together	47
	Formulation Structure – The Rule of Fours	*48*
	Cognitive & Processing Skills	*48*
	Academic Achievement	*49*
	Attention & Executive Functions	*50*
	Behavioural & Emotional Factors	*50*
	Health & Family Medical History Factors	*52*
	Social/Environmental Factors	*52*
7	Teach & Treat	55
	Teach	*55*
	Remediation	*55*
	The Science of Reading – Structured Literacy	*56*
	Content/What to Teach – The Basic Elements of Structured Literacy	*56*
	Instructional Practices – When and How to Teach	*57*
	Assessment – Diagnostic Teaching	*59*
	Accommodations	*60*
	Modifications	*62*
	Treat	*63*
	Attention Problems (ADHD)	*63*
	Behavioural/Emotional Challenges	*64*
8	Useful Resources	66
	References	*81*
	Index	*84*

Preface

Much research has been conducted in the field of reading challenges. Thousands of psychoeducational evaluations and screeners have been carried out with the goal of identifying individuals with dyslexia since Rudolph Berlin, a German ophthalmologist, first coined the term in 1887 (for a historical view of the development of research on dyslexia, you can refer to Kirby et al., 2020). Many professionals are interested and working in the field of dyslexia including educators, speech and language pathologists, psychologists, inclusion specialists, physicians and policy makers. Millions of individuals diagnosed with dyslexia around the world experience challenges with reading. Together with their parents, educators and professionals in the field they are forming groups, organizations, training centres, college and university programmes to address the needs of students diagnosed with dyslexia. When these reading difficulties are not identified and remediated they can have a devastating impact on the individual and society in general. Much progress has been made as a result of widespread dyslexia awareness campaigns and numerous laws enacted to address these challenges. Many screening tools and a plethora of intervention programmes to support individuals with dyslexia have been developed for schools and the workplace. Although the level of awareness, support and intervention varies depending on the country's resources, their language and the individual's community, information and services to address dyslexia have been definitely on the increase.

Given the increased awareness and understanding of dyslexia and its manifestations, we decided to write this book for you, teachers, using straightforward, non-technical language to make more accessible the descriptions of the process and background knowledge associated with dyslexia assessment. Our aim is to equip and empower you on the subject of dyslexia assessment. We hope to assist you in developing a "whole student" approach when considering dyslexia assessment. That is, our goal is to facilitate your understanding of all the factors that influence a student's learning. The better you understand the factors that impact reading, the types of evaluations, the steps in the assessment process, how to interpret the results and the different ways to develop and implement recommendations, the better prepared you will be to address the needs of students with dyslexia.

Our combined expertise in research and clinical practice in different parts of the world and from different professional perspectives have enabled us to develop a straightforward approach to the assessment of dyslexia that we call **"The LEFT Model"**. This logical, uncomplicated approach can be easily adopted by teachers when looking at the whole process of dyslexia assessment. We are very excited about the LEFT model's simplicity and are confident that it can enhance your skills to better understand the process of dyslexia screening and assessment. Furthermore, we also aim to increase your level of comfort when reviewing the psychoeducational evaluation reports that you encounter in your professional work. Our goal is that this book will provide you with the knowledge and skills to expand your understanding of the assessment process and allow you to discern which assessment reports are based on good practice from the ones that require additional rigour. It is our overarching desire to offer this approach that we believe will allow you to provide timely help and support for individuals diagnosed with dyslexia.

We are confident that the information we offer in this book will be very useful to most readers and we thank all teachers around the world for their endless efforts and continuous enthusiasm to support individuals with dyslexia and related disorders. This book is one of our efforts to do the same for individuals with dyslexia around the world by empowering teachers in the critical issue of dyslexia screening and assessment. We cannot help dyslexics if we do not identify them and assess them properly. Assessment is therefore the first important and critical step in this journey, and it is our wish and aim that this book enables you to do that.

Gad Elbeheri, PhD
Eric Q. Tridas, MD

1 The Nature of Dyslexia Assessment

Introduction & Definition

To provide an accurate assessment of dyslexia one must first offer an accurate operational definition. For how can we assess the existence of something if we do not know what it is? Dyslexia has enjoyed an immense interest from diverse stakeholders such as researchers, psychologists, educational administrators, parents, policy makers, physicians, teachers and individuals with dyslexia.

The term "dyslexia" was first coined by the German ophthalmologist Rudolph Berlin in 1887. Although it was first identified in medical circles, by the 1940s educational experts started to describe dyslexia by its different academic manifestations rather than the cause of the disorder. Along the way, various definitions of dyslexia were proposed as a direct result of the different disciplines and backgrounds of the individuals engaged in investigating this condition. Researchers with medical backgrounds define dyslexia as a condition resulting from neurological, neuromaturational and genetic causes. Structural and functional brain anomalies have been documented in dyslexics (Galaburda, 1989) as well as its genetic basis (Einarsdottir et al., 2017). It has been reported that dyslexia runs in families (Becker et al., 2017). Those in the field of psychology and education described it on the basis of the student's specific reading challenges rather than the medical origin of the problem. While the differences amongst persons with dyslexia are unique to the individual, the cause of dyslexia is neurological, the manifestations are behavioural, the diagnosis is clinical and the treatment is educational. This very complex nature of dyslexia has made the definition of the condition challenging. Thus, how dyslexia is defined may vary depending on the discipline describing it.

In our review of the research, it became evident that there are two main schools of thought that offer somewhat different definitions of dyslexia. One group narrowly defines the disorder as the results of deficits in reading mechanics in individuals with average to above average intelligence and appropriate educational experiences. We will refer to this group as "the splitters" as they separate and emphasize the elements that mostly impact reading. The other perspective looks at the clinical presentation of dyslexia and includes many of the coexisting challenges (also known as comorbidities) that, while not

DOI: 10.4324/9781003212058-1

necessarily the primary cause of the reading problems associated with dyslexia, often co-occur and have a dramatic impact on the individual's academic performance. We shall name this group "the lumpers" as they combine all the factors that impact dyslexia in their definition. The splitters narrow the scope of the problem (i.e., reading) which facilitates research in the mechanics of reading. The lumpers take a broader approach in their consideration of developmental dyslexia that includes wider aspects in the diagnosis and management of dyslexia and which reflects what is often observed.

For our own purposes, and being mindful of the important focus of this book, i.e., the assessment of dyslexia; we advocate the use of the dyslexia definition proposed by the International Dyslexia Association for the following reasons:

1. While there are many valid definitions of dyslexia (such as the ones adopted by the World Health Organizations (WHO), International Classification of Diseases (ICD-10), Diagnostic and Statistical Manual of Mental Disorders (DSM-5), the Health Council of the Netherlands, the British Dyslexia Association (BDA), etc., each one of these definitions is slightly different. This may lead us to various operational criteria that would complicate our goal of providing a straightforward understanding of the assessment of dyslexia. Thus, we have decided to focus on only one definition of dyslexia that enables us to concentrate on the nature of the assessment of reading skills and functions (the "splitters" approach). In addition, it allows us to provide a practical approach to assess the "whole individual" by considering other aspects of their clinical presentation (the "lumpers" perspective). Thus, our approach offers a roadmap for assessment that describes the structure of the evaluation and the specific elements to be assessed that aligns with the research and clinical presentation of the individuals with developmental dyslexia.
2. Established in 1949 as the Orton Dyslexia Society, the International Dyslexia Association is the oldest (more than 70 years old) and biggest non-profit dyslexia organization in the world with 45 branches in the US and Canada and 20 Global Partners. This US based international organization benefits from access and support of some of the most well-respected dyslexia experts in the world. Non-profit organizations such as the IDA enjoy both history and weight in the field of dyslexia. IDA concerns itself with the diverse types of dyslexia practitioners (e.g., educators, dyslexia therapists and diagnosticians) and seeks to disseminate and promote scientific based information regarding developmental dyslexia that has been shown to be effective in addressing the needs of individuals with dyslexia in all environments.
3. The definition of dyslexia below proposed by the International Dyslexia Association is not dissimilar to many other definitions, such as those offered by the WHO, DSM-5, ICD-10 as well as the British Dyslexia Association, for example. It provides the narrow focus of the functions impairing

the mechanics of reading (e.g., the phonological component of language) while acknowledging the consequences and coexisting factors that often impact the student's presentation. Adopted on November 12th, 2002, by IDA's Board of Directors[1] the definition is as follows:

Dyslexia is a specific learning disability that is neurobiological in origin. It is characterized by difficulties with accurate and/or fluent word recognition and by poor spelling and decoding abilities. These difficulties typically result from a deficit in the phonological component of language that is often unexpected in relation to other cognitive abilities and the provision of effective classroom instruction. Secondary consequences may include problems in reading comprehension and reduced reading experience that can impede growth of vocabulary and background knowledge.[2]

Dyslexia: Prevalence & Signs

The incidence of dyslexia varies significantly around the world and scientific publications provide varying statistics of the prevalence of dyslexia from 1.5% to 11% (Wagner et al., 2020). Differences in the phonology and orthography of a language and how different countries define and evaluate dyslexia can have an impact on these statistics. Reading, spelling, writing and language abilities exist on a continuum, as described in the IDA's Knowledge and Practice Standards for Teachers of Reading.

Decades of research and national test scores confirm that reading problems commonly occur and affect many individuals around the world. Dyslexia is the most common learning disorder representing 80% of all learning disabilities.[3] Approximately, one in five students of average to above average cognitive abilities and who are receiving typical instruction experience symptoms of dyslexia. Data provided by the National Assessment of Educational Progress (Reilly et al., 2019: NAEP) in the US reveal that approximately one third of fourth graders reading skills fall in the Below Basic classification. Such low literacy levels will prevent them from meeting the expectations of grade-level academic work. Adult literacy problems are also common, affecting one in four who are intelligent but have not been able to attain a functional literacy level.

The **key signs of dyslexia** include difficulty learning and using written language impacting *accurate word reading* (decoding and fluency) and *spelling*. Individuals with dyslexia experience trouble remembering letters and their sounds and struggle to read accurately and rapidly enough to comprehend. The difficulties processing and manipulating the sounds in the words, also known as *phonological awareness*, and specific language-based difficulties, such as *auditory memory* and *automatized naming*, are some of the underlying difficulties associated with dyslexia. Thus, the challenges of dyslexia are language-based and not the result of reading backwards, or low cognitive skills or intelligence. Other signs often observed in persons with dyslexia include problems organizing written and spoken work, learning a foreign language and memorizing math facts. Dyslexia occurs on a continuum and not all the individuals with these symptoms have dyslexia. However, when students continue to struggle with literacy skills, despite the provision of high-quality, evidence-based instruction, an assessment is needed to determine if they have dyslexia.

Early signs of dyslexia may include delays in developmental milestones related to language skills (understanding what others are saying or communicating with others), such as learning to talk, combining words into sentences or speaking clearly. Other early signs of dyslexia include struggling to learn the letter names and their corresponding sounds. Some students with dyslexia may not be very interested in listening to stories, although they may enjoy turning the pages and looking at the pictures. They may also avoid nursery rhymes or rhyming games.

By the time these students reach the **early primary grades** they begin to show more specific difficulties with reading, spelling and written communication when compared with their oral language skills. They may confuse sounds and experience trouble reading aloud, including poor expression (prosody). Given their decoding challenges, reading comprehension is often affected, despite having typical oral language development, including listening comprehension skills. Similarly, writing skills are often impacted. Other challenges include difficulties naming things rapidly (objects, colours, letters or numbers) and organizing their written and spoken language. Reading difficulties can impact other academic subjects too. For example, poor readers may struggle when attempting to solve math word problems as a result of their reading challenges. Similarly, research has shown that students diagnosed with dyslexia may also experience difficulty with number sense (also known as numerosity) and recalling math facts. In the early primary grades, many of the dyslexia coexisting problems tend to become more prominent. Difficulties with attention, handwriting, poor time tracking and behavioural and emotional dysregulation can become major challenges for these students. As a result, these individuals may become reluctant to go to school, develop behaviour problems such as tantrums or can become withdrawn and tearful.

Coexisting conditions are common in students with dyslexia. Many individuals diagnosed with dyslexia experience problems with language skills (listening comprehension and/or oral expression), attention, motor coordination, organization and mental math calculation. Other associated challenges include delays in learning how to dress themselves or doing up their buttons or buckles. They may also have a poor sense of time and difficulties with time concepts, like yesterday or next week, beyond four years of age. Some of them report having difficulty in learning common sequences, such as days of the week. While these challenges are not specific markers of dyslexia, they have a significant impact in the individual's performance and response to intervention and, thus, must be considered in the assessment of dyslexia.

As noted in the definition of dyslexia, secondary consequences include difficulties with reading comprehension, and development of vocabulary and general knowledge. Dyslexia may also result in other significant symptoms such as depression, anxiety, low self-esteem, school phobia and strained peer relationships (Giovagnoli et al., 2020). Children diagnosed with dyslexia tend to have lower self-concept than their peers. Poor literacy levels and weak general academic performance often leads to low self-esteem. Researchers have documented the association between self-concept, self-esteem and academic achievement (Livingston et al., 2018). Not all students who have difficulties with these symptoms have dyslexia. Formal assessment of reading, language and writing skills is an appropriate way to confirm a diagnosis of a student suspected of having dyslexia.

The signs of dyslexia are numerous and vary depending on the student. The International Dyslexia Association has excellent resources on its website regarding signs of dyslexia amongst other useful important information compiled into Fact Sheets. We encourage readers of this book and specially teachers to consult the website and download those extremely useful free resources.

Importance of Dyslexia Assessment

The assessment of dyslexia is one of the most important steps necessary to address the needs of a student with reading challenges because it is the first step in the formulation of the intervention and management plan. Dyslexia assessment holds the key for eligibility for special education services and for the assurance of specific rights, allowances, accommodations and modifications that students with dyslexia are entitled to receive based on relevant laws and regulations (Bell, 2013). The assessment should provide an explanation that will help the student understand the reasons for the challenges they experience at school. We refer to this as a "*demystification process*". Individuals of all ages diagnosed with dyslexia report that this process provides them with a sense of relief and reassurance that promotes self-confidence once they realize that their difficulties have a name and that it is a condition that can be managed, thus allowing them to become successful in their academic and work life. This process also diminishes the sense of guilt as students recognize that their challenges are not their fault. Without a proper assessment, it can become very difficult to differentiate between students with dyslexia and those who struggle with reading due to other factors. Because there are so many different reasons why students are not able to read and because reading is an essential skill to succeed in today's society; it is therefore vital to provide an accurate diagnosis of dyslexia so that those students are identified properly and as early as possible and supported so that barriers to their learning are removed (Reid & Guise, 2017).

Fundamentals of Dyslexia Assessment

An assessment is an information gathering process. If you would like to know if an individual has dyslexia, it is essential to gather information from different sources and synthesize it in a meaningful, practical manner that enables the teacher to make an informed decision about intervention (Mather & Wendling, 2012). The information gathered in the dyslexia assessment process can be distilled from various sources as we describe below.

1. *Parents:* Valuable information can be obtained from parents and other caregivers. Some of these data should include developmental milestones, educational, behavioural and social interaction history and relevant health, family and social history. This process will allow you to gather important and specific information about the student, including general family and environmental factors that may impact their presentation.
2. *Teachers*: Reviewing previous report cards, teacher's notes and having conversations with other teachers who are familiar with the student can supply valuable information about the student's leaning and behaviour. It provides a different perspective of the patterns of strengths and weaknesses, the individual's skills and the onset and duration of their challenges in school.
3. *The student*: Discussing with the individual their difficulties and strengths can generate a wealth of information. Students with learning challenges often understand that they have a problem but are not usually asked about their perspective. This is an opportunity to gain a more thorough understanding of the specific challenges the student is experiencing and a strategy to better connect with them.
5. *Current performance in school:* A general description of the child's performance in school, including their academic achievement as well as elements of conduct, behaviour and social interaction, should be an important component of the data. In addition, subject specific tests that are routinely administered in the classroom can provide invaluable information when performing error analysis.
6. *Current standardized measures:* Tests are one of the components of the assessment whereby specific instruments are used to gather information. All such information assembled is then converted into scores. Tests that quantify the individual's reading, writing, spelling and mathematical abilities are essential to the assessment of dyslexia. These assessments are often provided through *checklists, screening instruments, progress monitoring* and *formal psychoeducational evaluations*. Such information is then used to assist decisions regarding the best approach to intervention and eligibility for services that determine placement and the allocation of special education provisions.
7. *Current general cognitive skills & abilities:* Having an idea of the student's overall level of developmental functioning as well as specific processing strengths and challenges provides invaluable information about their learning. Descriptions of how the individual processes information including functions such as oral language, visual spatial abilities and phonological awareness, processing speed, memory abilities, attention, working memory and naming speed can provide a guide for the most appropriate intervention approach.

The quality and accuracy of the assessment process will depend on the educational level, specialized training, and years of experience of the professional(s) performing the evaluation and the instruments used to collect such information.

Types of Dyslexia Assessments

There are different types of dyslexia assessment instruments. Their application will depend on the ultimate purpose of the assessment. We have listed them for your review below.

1. *Checklists:* For the purposes of our book, we are defining checklists as *short, easy to administer instruments that do not include performing any tests*. They help identify children that may be *at risk for dyslexia*. They can be used by parents and teachers to document their observations and assist them on decisions about next steps if they suspect that the child may display dyslexia symptoms. Checklists are available in different formats including pen and paper or electronic. They are usually free of cost or very inexpensive. Checklists tend to be used widely in countries where there is limited or no available access to standardized psychometric tests (Hou et al., 2018). This form of assessment can provide some general information on the broad areas of difficulty experienced by the child. Checklists are most useful for the early identification of students at risk for dyslexia. Early identification, in turn, can lead to early intervention which has a greater impact when provided in the early primary grades (Snowling, 2013; Lovett et al., 2017). For example, a teacher may decide the child has a pronounced difficulty with word recognition. However, this does not provide information as to why this difficulty persists. We know that in order to read a child has to automatically recognize how the precise sequence of the sounds in a word matches a specific sequence of the graphemes (the letter or number of letters that represent a sound or phoneme), which in turn has a particular meaning. So, when assessing error patterns, you should be asking if the student has trouble with the orthographic (recognizing the precise order of the letters in a word), phonological (comparing the sequence of letters against their sounds), semantic (the meaning of the word) and context (general and topic knowledge, genre and text structure) processing systems. Therefore, as a teacher, you would be required to carry out further investigations to obtain some further explanations of the difficulty.

    Checklists are not designed to make a diagnosis of dyslexia. They should be used early on as a very first step to encourage early identification of students *at risk* for dyslexia. When a student is identified as being at risk for dyslexia, a referral for a comprehensive evaluation should be considered at that time. However, if the child's school has implemented an RTI model of identification and intervention, the student should then be provided with evidence based tiered support services.

2. *Screening Tests:* These instruments tend to be readily available for teachers, other professionals and sometimes, parents. For our purposes, *screening instruments include questions and limited testing of the individual*. Like checklists, screening instruments are intended to provide the user with a risk indicator of dyslexia rather than a diagnosis. They are cost effective and user friendly. As with the checklists, administration of screening tests can be done with pen and paper or electronically. Many of the screening tools are now available online. Some can be administered in a group setting while others are designed for individual use. If a student is identified as being at risk for dyslexia by a screening test, a full evaluation or progress monitoring through RTI is strongly recommended (Everatt et al., 2000). Screening tests save valuable time and are great for early identification purposes.

    Often a suspicion of the presence of difficulties can be identified through observation and screening assessments. Checklists and screeners are the first line of defence against dyslexia because they allow for the "structured" documentation of the symptoms and relevant information regarding observed behaviours frequently associated with dyslexia (Singleton et al., 2009). There are some important points to consider in relation to screening which include the following: The optimal age for individuals to be assessed, the underlying skills and functions to be tested and how to use the findings to guide next steps. While screening instruments can yield very useful information they should be used in conjunction with other data, including observations made by the teacher of the student's work and progress in different content areas of the curriculum.

3. *Comprehensive Evaluations:* These types of assessments tend to be conducted over several sessions so as not to overwhelm the individual being tested. They involve the administration of a number of psychometric instruments which aim to depict a more detailed picture about the individual's current cognitive profile as well as their academic achievement skills in reading, writing and spelling. Some of the cognitive functions assessed include language skills, visual spatial abilities, short term working memory, processing speed and rapid naming. Tests used in these evaluations tend to be psychometric in nature and are therefore more accurate and robust in their abilities to measure the underlying skills being tested. However, they take a much longer time to administer than screening tests and the evaluators must meet specialized licensing/certification requirements. This makes the administration of these types of assessment costly.

    At the conclusion of a comprehensive evaluation, a written report is usually provided to the individual or their parents. The report should include (1) a summary of the history, (2) test results, (3) a full explanation of the nature and findings of the evaluation and (4) the recommendations to address them. These types of assessments tend to be required by the school officials in order to ascertain the student's eligibility for educational support services. These interventions are often guaranteed by laws that would ensure the provision of accommodations, modifications and remediation services. There are issues pertaining to cultural fairness and linguistic appropriateness that must be satisfied when conducting such assessments, notably in cases of children coming from multilingual settings. Data collected during the assessment process is then put into context so that an overall picture of the individual's profile can be provided along with the necessary documentation for a diagnosis of dyslexia.

The evaluation of students with dyslexia can be performed by several different professionals. Standardized tests are usually administered by school psychologists, neuropsychologists, clinical psychologists, speech language pathologists and physicians. There are four major types of evaluations. These include (1) psychoeducational assessments, (2) psychological evaluations, (3) neuropsychological evaluations and (4) multidisciplinary evaluations. Each one of these types of assessments may include the administration of standardized tests, rating scales, direct observations of the child and a summary of the interviews with parents, teachers and the child. They typically include measures of intelligence, academic achievement, cognitive processes as well as behavioural and emotional concerns. It is important to note that the main difference between these types of assessments is based on the training and perspective of the examiner which, in turn, may change the purpose or focus of the evaluation.

Psychoeducational evaluations are typically performed by school psychologists and educational diagnosticians at the school to aid in determining if the student qualifies for special education services. Psychoeducational evaluations can be used to diagnose learning disorders and their underlying causes as well as determining if a student meets eligibility criteria for services.

Psychological evaluations are usually performed by clinical psychologists who often work in private practices. These types of evaluations aim to diagnose specific neurodevelopmental disorders, such as learning disorders, attention deficit-hyperactivity disorder (ADHD), autism spectrum disorders (ASD) and others. The focus of psychological evaluations is on diagnosis, but they can also be used for ascertaining eligibility for services at school.

Neuropsychological evaluations are administered by neuropsychologists, and they tend to be most comprehensive in nature. They emphasize how different brain functions impact the child's learning and behaviour. In other words, they focus on the cause of the student's challenges. This type of assessment is usually very comprehensive and evaluates in a more detailed fashion cognitive domains, such as executive functions, language, visual perceptual abilities, fine motor control, attention, adaptive skills, etc.

Multidisciplinary Evaluations are typically conducted by medical doctors, such as developmental and behavioural paediatricians, child neurologists and child psychiatrists, in conjunction with psychologists or neuropsychologists, educational diagnosticians, speech language pathologists, occupational therapists and other professionals. As their name implies, multidisciplinary evaluations provide different perspectives and findings from multiple professional disciplines. The goal is to provide a comprehensive report that attempts to address the cause of the student's challenges, the diagnosis(es) and provide data for the schools to determine if the student meets eligibility criteria for services.

Purpose of Dyslexia Assessment

An assessment of dyslexia is generally conducted for the following main purposes:

1. *To provide a clear indication of the individual's processing strengths and weaknesses, i.e., their cognitive profile:* The assessment of dyslexia can provide descriptions of the student's learning profile that can inform differentiated instruction. Different individuals learn differently and have varying patterns of strengths and weaknesses. Such information is extremely useful in the assessment process and in the intervention thereafter as it guides parents and teachers and aids their efforts in reaching the child with dyslexia in such a manner that ensures efficient processing. Teachers and parents can boost the strengths of students with dyslexia to keep them motivated while implementing a plan of intervention to strengthen their weaknesses. A dyslexia assessment makes this easier to do and clearer to see.
2. *To shed light on the individual's current level of academic achievement:* The assessment of dyslexia must lead to the quantification of the student's achievement gap. The greater the gap, the greater the likelihood that a more intense and longer duration of intervention(s) will be needed. This reading gap may vary from one student to another as dyslexia occurs in a continuum. Error analysis of the student's daily work and of standardized instruments administered during the assessment process can provide useful information to help you better understand their academic achievement challenges. The ultimate goal of intervention is to narrow this gap between the student's reading performance and that of their peers, hopefully raising the skills to an effective level. As indicated previously, this is typically accomplished by providing remediation and allowing for extra time for small group instruction.
3. *Provide an explanation for the student's difficulty with academic progress:* Regardless of the results of the assessment of dyslexia, it is always useful to understand why the student is experiencing a lack of progress. Academic achievement challenges can result from multiple factors beyond those specifically associated with dyslexia. For example, there can be cognitive, behavioural, medical and environmental issues that can significantly impact academic achievement. The findings of an assessment can also help identify elements of the curriculum that may challenge, motivate or discourage the student's progress. This can help the parents and teachers in ensuring that

the obstacles are properly addressed through accommodations, modifications and remediation. Helping students understand the reasons for their academic struggles can help address issues of self-concept and promote self-advocacy. In adults diagnosed with dyslexia their approach to overcome dyslexia related challenges may improve once they know the name and understand the nature of their difficulties.

4. *Identify specific diagnosis(es) and the features that define it:* This should facilitate ascertaining the student's eligibility for educational support services assured by the relevant laws and regulations and the provision intervention strategies. In addition, it provides a "name" for the difficulties that the person has allowing them to better understand their challenges.

5. *Inform and develop an Individual Educational Plan or "IEP" to guide the intervention process:* An assessment identifies the underlying strengths and weaknesses and quantifies the severity of the identified condition(s). These are all important factors when formulating an IEP (or the RTI process) to help the student overcome their challenges (Lindstrom, 2019). A major goal of the assessment of the student with dyslexia is to identify the most appropriate teaching and learning approaches. In other words, ***we test to inform how to teach!***

Notes

1 The focus of this book is on Developmental Dyslexia, i.e., a condition that some people have from birth. However, there is another rarer form of dyslexia referred to as acquired dyslexia, which occurs after an insult or a trauma to the brain. This book does not talk about acquired dyslexia.
2 https://dyslexiaida.org/definition-of-dyslexia
3 https://dyslexiaida.org/dyslexia-basics/

2 The LEFT Model
A Process for Dyslexia Assessment

Components of Dyslexia Assessment

Assessments are intended to gather information pertinent to a learning, developmental, behavioural, health and/or environmental concerns. They are based on multiple sources of data assembled from different settings. In order to accomplish this, the evaluators gather data by obtaining a history through interviews and/or questionnaires and testing. The **history** provides the qualitative data that describes the types of challenges the student is experiencing and the different domains of life that are affected by these factors. **Standardized tests** are another essential component of this process. They are intended to quantify the student's strengths and weaknesses described in the history by testing the functions and skills that impact learning. Therefore, standardized tests can tell us how serious a problem is (quantifying the problems with scores) and why it is happening (the profile of strengths and weaknesses based on scores). No decision should be based exclusively on a single test score. The goal of an assessment is to gather information to inform decisions, including meaningful recommendations.

To better understand our model for the assessment of dyslexia it may be helpful to begin with a "look from afar" or "bird's eye view". As we previously discussed, dyslexia is one of several learning disorders. In order for individuals to be diagnosed with a disorder they have to demonstrate that the symptoms that define it are causing impairment in one or more important life domains. Learning disorders can impact an individual's life in multiple domains, such as academic work, behaviour and emotional regulation, social relationships and health. Therefore, we should begin by identifying the main aspects of the student's life that are currently impacted. This is the "bird's eye view". For example, if we consider a student who presents with reading and spelling challenges, attention difficulties, excessive worrying, social isolation, sleep problems and frequent headaches, we can readily identify the domains that are impaired. These include their *academic performance* (reading and spelling challenges and attention difficulties), *behavioural/emotional regulation* (excessive worrying), *social relationships* (isolation) *and health* (sleep difficulties and headaches).

DOI: 10.4324/9781003212058-2

The Rule of Fours

Once we identify the domains that are impaired, we need to ascertain the functions and skills that are contributing to the student's challenges. Understanding the main contributing factors to the student's impairment will help guide the intervention plan. To simplify this process, we developed the **Rule of Fours.** This rubric allows you to identify the areas of impairment, the contributing factors, and the plan of intervention. We have summarized this in Figure 1.

Using the **Rule of Fours**, we should first identify the domains of functional impairment. These are as follows: (1) Academic/Occupational, (2) Behavioural/Emotional, (3) Social Interaction and (4) Health. It is important to remember that it is common for a student to experience challenges in more than one domain. Once you describe the areas of impairment, you can begin to focus on the factors that contribute to those challenges.

There are *four major contributing factors* to the individual's areas of impairment. These are the child's (1) ***developmental profile,*** (2) ***behaviour/emotional profile,*** (3) ***health factors*** and (4) ***the environment***.

1. The *developmental profile* describes the functions that impact learning, such as attention, mental age, processing speed, language skills, visual spatial abilities, tactile/kinaesthetic processing, executive functions, memory (short-term, working, and long-term) and motor control.
2. The *behaviour profile* describes the individual's behaviour and emotional symptoms by dividing them into three main categories: Internalizing disorders (e.g., anxiety, and depression), externalizing disorders (e.g., oppositional-defiant and conduct disorders) and atypical disorders (e.g., autism spectrum disorders).

CONTRIBUTING FACTORS	**AREAS OF DEFICITS**	**TYPES OF INTEVENTION**
1. Developmental Profile		1. Academic
2. Behaviour Profile	1. Academic 2. Behavioural/Emotional 3. Social Relationships 4. Health	2. Psychological
3. Health		3. Medical
4. Environment		4. Environmental

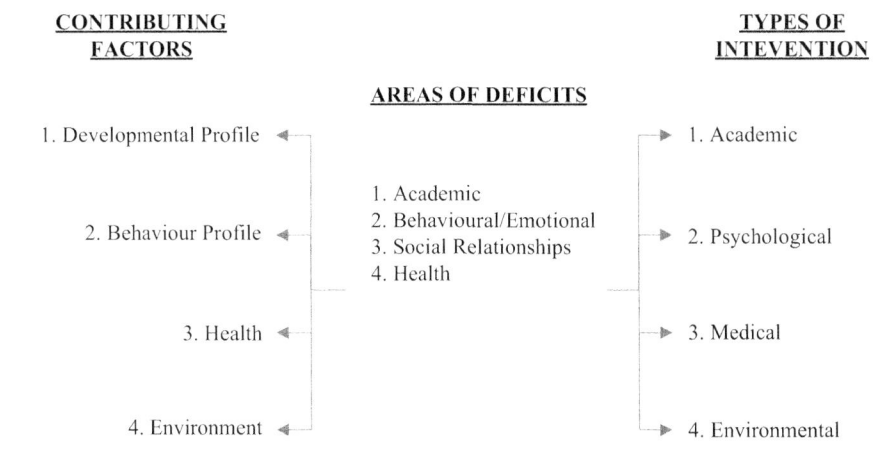

Figure 1 The Rule of Fours

3. There are general *health* factors that can impact learning. Many health conditions, sleep problems and medical treatments can affect a student's academic and behavioural performance.
4. Finally, we look at the *environment* as it has a dramatic impact on the student's life. We generally consider three general environments in the individual's life which are as follows: (1) Student's home, (2) student's school and (3) student's peers. A family history of learning and/or behavioural/emotional disorders can suggest a possible genetic predisposition to disorders like dyslexia, ADHD and anxiety. Environmental stressors can also have a dramatic effect in the student's learning; therefore, it is critical to identify them. The language spoken at home can also have an impact on the student's learning. A critical environmental school factor to consider is the curriculum expectations. School systems have three main goals for all their students: (1) Acquisition of literacy skills, (2) general knowledge and (3) preparation for adult life (higher education, technical school or work). Knowing the student's current grade provides invaluable insight on what skills need to be included in the assessment process. Providing teachers with access to the necessary history and formal and informal assessments, will allow them to determine the most appropriate approach to intervention.

Once we have ascertained the factors that cause impairment we can then focus on their management. Any type of intervention can be grouped into four major categories: (1) **Educational management**, (2) **psychological management**, (3) **medical management** and (4) **environmental management**.

1. *Educational management* is provided through three general approaches. These include the following: Remediation, accommodations and modifications. *Remediation* requires the provision of science-based instruction delivered with fidelity and sufficient intensity to strengthen the student's weaknesses and allow them to "catch up". This is usually done in small group or one-to-one instruction, as in the case of Response to Intervention Model "RTI" or through special education programmes that provide specialized instruction by teachers with expertise in the field of dyslexia and other learning disorders. Some other common remedial interventions include speech language, occupational and/or physical therapies. *Accommodations*, on the other hand, take advantage of the students' strengths to help them overcome their weaknesses. For example, the use of assistive technology, such as text-to-voice software, or providing a reader allows individuals with dyslexia who have strong listening comprehension skills listen to text or test questions. This is particularly helpful when trying to evaluate knowledge in a particular field rather than skills, such as reading and writing. Extended time on testing is another common accommodation. *Modifications* are a type of accommodation that can impact the volume of work that a student produces. For example, cutting back the number book reports that a student must complete for a course is a common modification that is

provided in the K–12 years. However, it is not offered in higher education as this would impact diploma requirements.
2. *Psychological management* is generally provided by psychologists and mental health counsellors. However, in the classroom, teachers often must address behaviour and emotional challenges. In general, there are two main types of approaches to psychological interventions: Behaviour modification and cognitive behaviour therapy. *Behaviour modification* is generally used to address the needs of children with externalizing disorders, like oppositional defiant disorder (ODD) and neurodevelopmental disorders like ADHD. This approach is mostly focused on the adults. That is, the adults change the way that they manage the child's behaviour and, as a result, the child changes the way that they respond to the adult. In this situation, the factors that regulate the behaviour are external to the child. There are many behavioural programmes designed for classroom implementation. *Cognitive behaviour therapy* (CBT) is typically implemented in the management of internalizing disorders, like anxiety and depression. Unlike behaviour modification, the goal of CBT is to help individuals change the way that they think about how they feel. Teachers can learn some of these strategies that may help address the needs of some of their students by reviewing the recommended readings in the resource section of this book.
3. *Medical interventions* are well beyond the scope of a teacher's classroom. However, medical doctors often rely on teachers' feedback to ascertain the efficacy of a particular medication or its dose. This is often the case in the management of ADHD and other common neurobehavioural disorders.
4. *Environmental interventions* are often implemented in schools. These may include preferential seating or taking tests in a separate classroom, and/or in untimed conditions. More significant environmental interventions may require placement of a student in a school that specializes in the instruction of students with varying learning needs. Similarly, adjusting in the structure and routine of a home or classroom environment can have a very dramatic impact on a child.

The LEFT Model

To simplify the steps described above into one meaningful model that teachers can easily follow, we developed the acronym **LEFT**. This strategy allows you to identify and remember the four major components of a typical dyslexia assessment. These steps include obtaining a *history*, *testing the student*, *interpretation of the findings* and *formulating a teaching and treatment plan*. In the LEFT model the letters stand for the following:

1. *Listen*: Refers to taking a good history.
2. *Evaluate*: Refers to the use of standardized and qualitative instruments to measure observed cognitive, academic and behavioural symptoms.

3. *Formulate:* Refers to integrating the history with the test findings in order to explain the student's challenges and help direct intervention.
4. *Teach/Treat:* Refers to the provision of science based educational, behavioural, cognitive and medical interventions to improve academic progress and student wellbeing.

Below we give a detailed description of each component of our LEFT Model.

Listen: History

The most important step in conducting an assessment is to identify the strengths and challenges in a student which should help guide the instructional approach. If you want to know what challenges a student has, all you need to do is ask. Ask the student, the parents, previous teachers and other professionals who have met the child. This will help you understand what the early characteristics were, how the student has responded to different interventions and what are the current needs to be addressed. A critical component of listening is to emphasize *observable behaviours*, rather than opinions. Let us consider the case of a second-grade student who has reading and spelling challenges and shows extreme shyness and social withdrawal. This child also has attention difficulties and complains of stomach aches and headaches on a regular basis. This student may have several different conditions that often present together (frequently referred to as comorbidities), or perhaps some of these manifestations are triggered by one primary disorder. A structured, thorough history can help a teacher sort through these observations and will allow them to better understand the condition.

It is very important for teachers during this *Listening* stage to remember that it would be more appropriate not to focus on the question *"what does the student have?"* but rather **describe what you and others have observed**. It is always important to remember that at the end, all that is managed are the symptoms that contribute to the student's impairment. Thus, we recommend that during this stage of the assessment process it is best to identify the symptoms as they can provide an explanation for the described difficulties, rather than labelling or diagnosing the child. Getting a complete picture of the student's strengths and weaknesses over time will help identify the areas that need remediation as well as the strengths that can help a student succeed in school and adult life. Once the main areas of concern have been identified, it is helpful to document the repetitive themes and patterns of challenges and successes experienced by the student since they first enrolled in a school setting, starting with the pre-school years and ending with the present day. We shall discuss later in greater detail how to classify the signs and gather information from other sources to guide the assessment. Listening to what the parents, students and other professionals describe will help strengthen your interactions with them and facilitate communication.

Evaluate: Testing and Documentation

The purpose of testing is to quantify the observations described in the history. By obtaining a good history, one has already begun to identify a student's pattern of strengths and weaknesses. A test can help measure how significant a weakness or a strength the student has. This is similar to having a child in your classroom whose skin is flushed, feels warm to touch and has a runny nose. Taking the student's temperature will tell you how high the fever is, but it does not give you a diagnosis. The higher the fever, the greater the concern. However, you already knew the child was sick because of what you observed. Taking his temperature helped you quantify the severity of his problem. Let us now follow the same analogy for reading challenges. A teacher can measure the degree of difficulty of a student who struggles with word attack skills and spelling through **progress monitoring**. By working individually with a child on their classwork, it is possible for a teacher to identify the elements of reading that the student struggles with when doing an **error analysis**. Tests used for progress monitoring can also help quantify the student's academic performance and document their progress. Performing an error analysis of the daily work can complement the tests that are administered as part of the evaluation. In the coming chapters we shall discuss examples of the teacher's role in the assessment process and some of the instruments and strategies available to facilitate it.

Another way to objectively assess a child is by performing a **psycho-educational or neuropsychological evaluation**. These assessments are administered by highly trained professionals. However, like progress monitoring, all these tests do is quantify the student's functions and academic achievement skills level. These evaluations are performed for different reasons. In most school systems, psycho-educational evaluations are used to ascertain if a student meets eligibility criteria for educational support services. This is different than an assessment used for a diagnostic evaluation, which is intended to provide a diagnosis and an explanation of the student's challenges, even if the child is not eligible for educational support services. All these assessments can help identify the functions and skills that combine to contribute to a student's impairment. They may provide an explanation or perspective of the student's strengths and weaknesses which, in turn, will help guide differentiated instruction. In other words, ***testing should inform instruction***. The teacher can use the data provided by the assessment to guide the instructional approach for that student. When interpreting tests, it is important to consider how they measure a particular skill or function as this varies from one instrument to another. For example, reading comprehension can be measured in one test by using a cloze procedure (fill in the blanks) while another uses a multiple-choice format. A third test may allow the student to refer to the text when giving an answer while others may not. Recognizing these differences can provide the teacher with greater understanding of the test results and how these can guide instruction. We shall provide more details in the coming chapters regarding a practical approach to interpreting psychoeducational evaluation results.

Formulate: Putting It All Together

The primary reason to perform an assessment is to guide instruction. To accomplish this, the findings should be presented in a clear fashion. The analysis of the data should provide documentation and a clear explanation for the challenges that the student is experiencing in school. This analysis should be documented in a clear and organized manner that provides the supporting data for the specific diagnosis(es) made during the assessment. There should be a description of the different functions that affect an academic skill. In the case of a student who is struggling with reading, the assessment should provide a description of the functions that are impacted and the academic skills that have been affected by those functions. As such, the formulation should describe how factors, like phonological problems, rapid automatized naming weakness, oral language challenges or attention difficulties are impacting reading and writing skills. Another important component of the evaluation is to ascertain whether the student meets diagnostic criteria for one or more disorder(s). In our experience, every assessment should answer five fundamental questions:

1. Does the student have a problem (or problems)?
2. What is the name of that (those) problem(s) (diagnosis-diagnoses)?
3. What causes it (them)?
4. What can be done about it (them)?
5. What can be expected in the future?

Answering only one or two of those questions is not sufficient to implement a successful intervention plan. Every individual who has a diagnosis of dyslexia will likely experience reading and spelling challenges, however they will differ significantly from one another. The educational approach used for a child with a serious phonological problem will differ from that of a child who has a rapid automatized naming weakness or an oral language problem. Similarly, if this student also has an attention deficit hyperactivity disorder or a generalized anxiety disorder, their learning may be impacted by them to a significant extent. That is why **understanding all the variables** that can impact the student's presentation is essential to formulate an appropriate plan of instruction. In other words, *if you have a good description of the symptoms contributing to the student's problems, you can formulate a good educational prescription to address them.*

Teach/Treat

Once the evaluation is completed, a differentiated instructional approach must be developed for every student. When the teacher has a clear understanding of the developmental functions (such as phonological awareness, rapid automatized naming, oral language, attention, etc.) that are impacting specific reading skills, they can then formulate a plan of instruction. In the classroom, teachers can provide three major types of interventions:

1. Educational
2. Behavioural/emotional
3. Environmental

The **educational interventions** can be divided into *remediation, accommodations and modifications*. Remediation strategies focus on the student's weaknesses. The goal of this type of intervention is to strengthen the individual's weaknesses in order to narrow the gap between the student's current academic performance and that of their peers. That is, remediation should allow the student to "catch up". This will require an accelerated rate of learning which is accomplished by providing more time for instruction and supervised practice in a small group setting. *Accommodations*, on the other hand, focus on the student's strengths to help them overcome their weaknesses. *Modifications* are adaptations of the curriculum designed to adjust the work production demands based on the student's abilities. Most teachers are already familiar with many of these three types of intervention strategies which are often implemented as part of differentiated evidence-based instruction. While they are essential for students with dyslexia, they are beneficial to every child. We shall provide a more detailed description of these approaches to intervention in the coming chapters.

3 Listen

As we previously discussed, the dyslexia assessment is essentially an information gathering process. To document the symptoms of dyslexia and related disorders, we need to collect as much information as possible. Descriptions of the student in their natural learning environment, the classroom and at home are therefore extremely important to inform this process. A vital source of information is the history that can be obtained from the student, parents, caregivers and previous teachers. This data should include a brief description of the domains in the child's life that are being impacted, including academic work, behaviour and emotional regulation, social relationships and health, based on the type of impairment described in our Rule of Fours (see Chapter 2).

Before beginning the interview process, you may want to describe some of the student's strengths and weaknesses that you have observed in school and ask the parents if they have noticed a similar pattern of indicators at home. In our experience, when talking with parents, it may be helpful to begin the discussion by describing what you have observed in school, rather than what you think is the problem. You can then explain that the child seems to be having difficulties in specific domains and that you want to ensure that they succeed at school.

Once the above general concerns have been reviewed, you may start gathering a targeted history with the goal of identifying the factors that are contributing to the child's impairment based on the Rule of Fours. As such, the history should include information regarding the student's developmental and behavioural/emotional profile, health factors and the environment. It is important to know if these observed signs are present in other situations to ensure that they are not specific to one environment, such as school or home. It is also of the utmost importance to identify areas of strengths because these can help improve the child's sense of self-worth and provide an avenue for facilitating their learning and success in the future. Given that most children diagnosed with dyslexia present with other coexisting conditions, it is critical to obtain a more detailed history in order to understand how to best address the student's challenges.

The interview may also be a good opportunity to find out from the parents what strategies they have found effective in addressing some of their child's concerns at home. You too can share the tactics that you have found beneficial in tackling the student's challenges at school. An important goal is for you to help parents understand that you are not blaming them for their child's difficulties or that they have failed their child. The goal of the "Listening" process is to allow the parents the opportunity to see you as their ally in addressing their child's challenges and as someone who cares and who is trying to help.

The Educational History: Developmental Profile and Academic Work

Academically, children with dyslexia can be at a major disadvantage when compared with typical readers. Many of these students begin to demonstrate difficulties in infancy and before they enter school. Children with a history of language and articulation delays are at higher risk for dyslexia. Children who do not understand what they hear cannot understand what they read! Articulation difficulties and rhyme insensitivity can indicate a phonological processing problem. Delays in letter recognition and letter/sound association are some of the core deficits in dyslexia, therefore it is critical to inquire about these skills. Similarly, receptive and expressive language abilities are essential for reading. Questions such as "Can the child understand what is read to them?" and "Can the child read effortlessly?" or "Can the child describe an event or retell a story accurately?" are helpful in shedding light about these skills.

Obtaining a history of the acquisition and development of oral language and literacy skills will provide the foundation for determining the most appropriate standardized tests to be used in the assessment of a student with dyslexia. There are obvious early markers that can help identify children who are at high risk for developing dyslexia. Those early markers may subsequently manifest as specific reading problems as the child grows and moves from preschool to early primary grades. For example, a child who has a history of delayed language milestones, rhyming insensitivity, difficulty with letter recognition/identification and letter/sound association problems is at a very high risk for developing dyslexia. When eliciting the child's developmental history, you may want to refer to the Early Developmental and Academic Questionnaire on the Resource section of this book.

Once the child enters the early years of primary school, more specific information can be gathered about academic skills. You may want to inquire about difficulties with word attack skills, such as sounding out unfamiliar words or the rapid and accurate word recognition. Spelling is an excellent indicator of phonological processing challenges. Similarly, students who struggle learning sight words are likely to experience reading challenges. Comparing the student's reading performance with some of their other skills, such as arithmetic, may also help identify specific areas of academic challenge. As students move on in school, they may experience greater difficulty completing reading and writing assignments. Content subjects, such a social studies or literature may be more difficult for students to achieve due to their reading challenges. Similarly, as word problems in math are introduced, students with reading challenges may struggle with math problem solving.

Assessment of attention problems is also crucial when conducting an interview as it is one of the most common coexisting conditions in students diagnosed with dyslexia. Children with ADHD tend to have decreased productivity and accuracy of schoolwork. Because of their challenges with inattention, impulsivity and hyperactivity, they may complete less academic work than their classmates and have a propensity to make careless mistakes. Unlike students who have symptoms of dyslexia, those with ADHD do not have a skill deficit. Rather, they struggle with work completion and accuracy. The impact of ADHD in executive functions is well documented and can have a dramatic effect on reading comprehension. Hence, if you want to be able to address the academic challenges of students with dyslexia, you must also inquire about possible attention problems.

With this information at hand, you have a fairly good idea of the developmental functions and academic challenges the student is experiencing. For example, children who easily understand what a teacher reads (listening comprehension) but cannot comprehend what they read, (because of difficulties with word attack skills such as decoding and fluency) have classical signs of dyslexia. A child who has excellent word attack skills, but poor listening comprehension, is likely to have an oral language disorder. And a student who is very inconsistent in their performance may have an attention problem.

Behaviour/Emotional Regulation

Behaviourally and emotionally, dyslexia can have a significant negative effect on a child's self-esteem. It is often said that confidence comes from competence. Thus, it would be most difficult for a child who struggles on a daily basis with reading and writing to feel confident about their academic work, especially reading. This can leave emotional scars that can last a lifetime, even in successful adults.

As discussed in Chapter 2, there are three main patterns of human behaviour: Internalizing, externalizing and atypical patterns. Internalizing and externalizing behaviours are considered "normal" and exhibited by most children and adults throughout their lives. They are only considered a disorder if the symptoms occur with enough frequency and severity to impair any of the four domains listed in the Rule of Fours (e.g., schoolwork, behaviour and emotional regulation, peer interactions and health). Atypical behaviours, on the other hand, are disorders of quality not quantity. As the word implies, these patterns of behaviour are not typical as most children do not display them. Atypical symptoms affect how people interact, communicate and behave.

Beginning with preschool, you should inquire about the student's behaviour at school – general questions such as: "Did the child have trouble sitting at circle time?"; "Was the student easily distracted or inattentive?"; "Were there any indications of noticeable shyness and/or withdrawal?"; "Did the child appear reticent to interact with other students or was extremely shy?"; "Was this child defiant and/or aggressive?"; "Was there an unusual quality to the way the student communicated or interacted with others?" Internalizing disorders, such as anxiety and depression, are often reported in individuals with learning challenges. These types of disorders can result from or can be aggravated by long-standing school difficulties. Other students may choose to act out. Students with an autism spectrum disorder may struggle with inference, figurative language and extrapolation given their pragmatic language skills difficulties. Those who display oppositional and defiant symptoms may be reacting to academic or environmental challenges.

Health

While this is a topic that teachers do not usually inquire about, it may shed light on some of the factors that can impact the child's observed symptoms. In multidisciplinary clinics and many public schools, this information is gathered by physicians, school nurses, social workers and/or psychologists, rather than teachers. However, not every school has access to these professionals, which may provide important information that can help understand the challenges that a particular student or family is experiencing. Explaining this to the family and ensuring that the questions are general in nature may allow teachers to recommend further exploration of some of these health and environmental factors by other professionals.

Health problems can place a student at risk for learning challenges. Factors, such as pregnancy complications, premature birth, chronic illnesses, sleep difficulties and taking some medications can have a dramatic effect on the child's learning and behaviour regulation. In addition, there are some medical problems that occur with a higher frequency in children diagnosed with dyslexia and related disorders. Problems such as day or night-time wetting (enuresis) and bowel accidents (encopresis) occur ten times more frequently in children with learning and behavioural disorders than in the general population. Some of the general information that should be gathered includes the following:

- *Complications during pregnancy, labour, delivery or new-born period:* These can place a child at a higher risk for developmental and behavioural disorders. The way we would recommend this inquiry is to ask, *"Were there any major concerns before, during or after birth?"* There is no need to know the specific problems. You can explain to the parents why you are requesting this information. If you learn there were issues or complications, you can then recommend that the parents consult with the child's physicians to see if any of these factors could contribute to the learning and/or behaviour symptoms that the child is displaying.
- *Developmental history:* Special focus on early language milestones and motor development during the first two years of life is very important. This information can provide documentation of early indicators of reading challenges. Once again, the questions should be very general, e.g., "Did your child experience any delays in any of the following":
  - Speech (pronunciation of words)
  - Language (vocabulary, sentence construction, understanding what they heard, etc.)

- Motor coordination (sitting, walking, playing sports, using silverware, dressing, e.g., buttoning, snapping, zipping, etc.)

As indicated previously, these questions do not need to be extremely specific, but if the parents acknowledge any possible delays in these developmental milestones, it may be necessary to recommend further evaluations from a speech language pathologist, occupational and/or physical therapists.

- *Chronic health concerns:* Chronic and significant illnesses can impact the student's energy level, attention span and overall ability to perform. These conditions may also result in inconsistent school attendance or extended absences. There is no need to request detailed medical information. This should be handled in the same manner as the pregnancy and birth related questions.
- *Medications:* Some medications can cause changes in mood, energy or state of alertness. This would have a significant effect in the student's academic performance. Therefore, it is particularly important to provide documentation if a child develops a sudden change in behaviour or academic performance following a particular medical treatment. For example, many students who experience asthma are treated with medications that can make them irritable and/or anxious. Therefore, if the student is taking any medications (no need to know which medicines the child is taking), the teacher may want to encourage parents to consult with the prescribing physician to ensure that these medicines are not having a significant negative impact in their developmental or behavioural performance or may be contributing to some of the symptoms that are being observed.
- *Family History:* Research has demonstrated that dyslexia and other neurodevelopmental and neurobehavioural disorders, run in families. Therefore, it is important to inquire if the child has a close family member (parents, siblings, grandparents and/or aunts/uncles) with a history of reading difficulties, as this would place them at a higher risk for dyslexia. As with other aspects of the medical history, this is not information that is often shared with teachers. However, it is essential that this is documented as part of the evaluation as it has tremendous importance in the child's overall presentation. In our experience, many parents report similar experiences when they were attending school. A strategy that we implemented in our clinics included asking the parents *"Does your child remind you of anyone in the family?"*. It is not necessary to identify the person, just the presence of learning and behaviour challenges in relatives.

Environment

When considering environmental factors that impact the child, we focus on three main ones: *School, home and the peer group.*

- *School*: As noted previously, students diagnosed with dyslexia are at a great disadvantage in the school environment. Educational systems have three main goals for their students: (1) Acquisition of basic academic skills (reading, writing and arithmetic), (2) general education and (3) preparation for adult life. Thus, there will be different developmental expectations and demands placed on the student depending on their grade level. The time to learn to read is from prekindergarten to third grade. From the fourth grade on the students are reading to learn. It is well documented that after the third-grade children acquire most of their vocabulary and general knowledge through reading. Children who are diagnosed with dyslexia and related disorders and who have not received appropriate remediation will not be able to read as well as their peers. Therefore, they do not have the necessary skills to meet the work expectations of the late elementary (fourth and fifth grade), middle and high school years, not to mention college and adult life. From the fourth grade on, the educational expectations of almost every school system in the world emphasize the acquisition of general information (content subjects), rather than basic literacy skills (reading, writing and arithmetic). Thus, the focus of the educational system shifts from developing skills to applying them. That is why early identification is so critical. Similarly, understanding how the academic demands change from one educational stage to the next may help guide the intervention process. It is also important to recognize that some of the coexisting conditions that often accompany dyslexia can have a different impact based on the curriculum demands. For example, organization and planning become critical skills needed for success after the third grade. In middle school the child must juggle multiple teachers and a higher level of social competencies which can impact academic performance to a significant degree. Thus, students diagnosed with ADHD or experiencing executive function problems may have greater difficulties than those who do not have these challenges.

- *Home*: The home environment can have a dramatic impact in a student's performance. However, like the medical history, this is not a topic that parents are always comfortable discussing with teachers. However, this information can be of critical importance in understanding the student's challenges. There are three main areas that can provide some insight into the home life. These are (1) parent-child relationship, (2) efficacy of discipline or parenting and (3) level of family stress. One strategy that we have used over the years that provides us with a picture of what the student's day-to-day life is like at home is to review a typical school day for the child. It provides an opportunity to gain an understanding of the structure of the child's day at home and may offer insight into challenges associated with ADHD, executive functions, homework, fine motor control, sleep and different aspects of family life. For example, having a parent describe a morning routine will offer an opportunity to learn how rested the child is by asking how difficult it is to wake them up. Fine motor control is needed for dressing (buttoning, snapping, tying and zipping) as well as handling silverware at breakfast.

Discipline efficacy and behaviour management can help identify another area of concern that may need to be addressed. The main question to ask pertains to the efficacy of behaviour management at home and the child's level of *compliance*. In other words, *how easily can parents get the child to do what they want them to do, when they want them to do it.*

Another delicate topic that must be covered as part of the history of the student is environmental stress. As with other sensitive and confidential information covered in this section, it is not important to document details. Rather, a general inquiry about major life experiences is all that is needed. We suggest providing a list of such instances (e.g., birth of a child, death of a relative, health concerns of relatives, loss of a job, marital difficulties, divorce or a move/relocation) and ask the parents if any of these situations, or other events, have occurred in the last year. Emphasize that all you need to ascertain is if there are other unexpected factors in the child's life that may impact their current presentation.

- *Peer group:* The student's peer group exerts a significant influence on their functioning, particularly in middle and high school. Seeking peer acceptance becomes a primary driving force for adolescents and this can impact their academic work, behaviour and health. This grants a significant degree of influence over the child's life that often supersedes adult approval. Seeking peer acceptance will become a primary force in the child's life during the adolescence and young adult years.
- The **social interaction history** offers a window into the child's ability to self-regulate. Teachers are in a unique position to assess social interaction because they have age and grade appropriate "control subjects" for comparison in the classroom. This special opportunity allows teachers to have a good understanding of a child's social cognition and pragmatic language skills. It can also help identify behaviour patterns that impact social relationships, such as anxiety, depression, ADHD, oppositional and conduct disorders. In addition, observing a child's interaction with peers provides an invaluable opportunity to assess the child's ability to process higher level language reasoning skills in a non-academic situation. It is also important to recognize that peer acceptance is a great indicator of future success. A brief inquiry on the student's ability to make and keep friends is quite helpful. In addition asking about the age of peers with whom they get along best is useful data. An understanding of their level of empathy, sense of fairness and sportsmanship can shed light on their ability to understand others and their social skills.

4 Evaluate

Teacher Assessment of Language & Literacy

Teachers play a pivotal role in the dyslexia assessment process. As we highlighted before, teachers are great observers of their students and their points of strengths and weaknesses. Teachers are trained to identify reading difficulties by observing their students inside and outside of the classroom. This places them in a unique position to collaborate with the special needs educators and coordinators in their school, with the school psychologist or the local educational authority, psychologist and/or the parent. This facilitates their ability to gather further information and provide observations to help identify students who are at risk for or diagnosed with dyslexia. Once the findings are documented and analysed, teachers can then proceed to design a remediation and support plan to implement in school for their students with reading challenges, including dyslexia.

In addition to their very important role in providing educational intervention for their students with dyslexia, teachers also play another essential role in the assessment process. Although most teachers are not trained or licensed to provide cognitive assessments, they can use many other tools available to them to assist in the dyslexia assessment process. As previously mentioned, checklists or screeners can be used as initial probes that teachers are able to perform with ease in individual or group settings, using an online format or in a conventional paper and pencil instrument. In addition, there are also a number of tests available for teachers to use, after receiving appropriate training, which can aid in the dyslexia assessment process.

In order to facilitate the type of observations and selecting the type of screening instruments that teachers use it may be helpful to review the sequence of how their students acquire reading skills. Ehri (1995) describes five stages of reading which coincide with the developmental stages of their oral language skills and the type of instruction that students receive in each grade. The preschool students begin with an awareness of words within sentences. Subsequently (late pre-K and early kindergarten) they begin to notice syllables and onset sounds while beginning to acquire letter recognition. These early stages are followed by other reading skills such as letter-sound correspondence and phoneme blending and segmentation (late K to early first). Later in the first grade, they become familiar with word parts and word families and finally they attain reading fluency. All of these skills are necessary to fulfil the ultimate goal of reading comprehension. Each one of these phases should be mastered before proceeding to the next. This knowledge is essential in order to effectively teach and remediate the specific skills, at the proper time and in the most appropriate manner. Capitalizing on this understanding, teachers can use instruments that would assess these skills based on the student's grade level. The checklist provided by Houston in the book *The Dyslexia Assessment* (Reid & Guise, 2019), described in the next section, is an excellent example of such an instrument.

Another way to screen for these types of problems is to implement a *Root Cause Analysis* as described by the Lastinger Centre for Learning at the University of Florida. In this model, your decisions about intervention are based on screening data. If we use Ehri's five stages of reading model, the student's grade determines the type of skill screening to perform. If the student does not reach a benchmark, you should evaluate a previous skill to ensure that this is not the root cause of the problem. For example, if a student is in the first grade you would assess for decoding skills. If they pass the benchmark, then you can evaluate for fluency, the next skill in the sequence. If the student fails the decoding screening, you can then assess for phoneme blending and decoding of simple Consonant-Vowel-Consonant (C-V-C) words. If they fail that screener, that would indicate that you have to provide intervention at the phonemic awareness level.

This model is also applicable for students in 5th grade or older, where this reverse process can be used to determine the skills that need intervention. Let us consider the case of a 6th grade child who is administered a screener to assess reading comprehension. If they fail the reading comprehension screener, the teacher can then assess the reading skills in reverse order, that is fluency, word families and word parts, decoding and phonemic awareness to identify the skills that will need intervention.[1]

Checklists for Teachers[2]

There are different checklists for identifying students at risk for dyslexia. Checklists, however, need to be treated with considerable caution. They are not designed to make a definitive diagnosis of dyslexia, but they can help identify students that are at higher risk for reading and other developmental problems and who may need a more comprehensive assessment. Checklists can also provide information of some the student's strengths and weaknesses. Checklists can also be used to monitor the child's progress.

Examples of Checklists

Nursery Stage (3–6 Years Old)

- Poor language and pronunciation
- Poor rhyming
- Immature speech pattern and communication

- Poor letter knowledge
- Poor phonological awareness
- Poor concept of time
- Poor organization
- Poor listening skills
- Poor memory for rhymes, stories, events, instructions
- Cannot clap a rhythm or keep a musical beat
- Clumsy, wriggly and accident prone
- Hard to engage, shows little interest in activities
- Can be easily distracted
- Has poor posture
- Poor fine motor skills, including drawing, copying and letter formation
- Poor spatial concepts
- Poor body image
- Has not established hand dominance
- Has poor ball skills
- Has poor balance and co-ordination
- Social skills are very limited or unsuccessful

Lower Primary Stage (5–8 Years Old)

- Finds it hard to learn letter/sound relationships
- Confuses letters or words with similar shapes or sounds
- Finds it hard to sound out simple words
- Reverses, inserts or omits words, letters and numbers
- Has difficulty with spelling very simple regular words
- Muddles the order of letters and words
- Keeps losing the place when reading
- Reads and does written work very slowly
- Has difficulty pronouncing longer common words
- Has difficulty hearing rhymes and sounds within words
- Has poorly spaced, poorly formed, large faint or small heavily indented writing
- Has difficulty memorising (especially in number work) despite adequate supported in-school practice
- Slow to learn to tell the time
- Slow to learn to tie shoelaces
- Confuses left/right and up/down
- Has difficulty learning the alphabet, months and days in order
- Has delayed or idiosyncratic speech and language development
- Has difficulty carrying out an oral instruction or, more commonly, multiple oral instructions
- Has poor organising ability – losing and forgetting things
- Has poor coordination and depth perception – tripping and bumping into things
- Has word finding difficulties
- Behaviour difficulties, frustration, poor self-image

- Easily distracted – either hyperactive or daydreaming
- Other – please give detail

It is important to reiterate that class teachers are not expected to be able to diagnose dyslexia, but some general indications are listed below. If several of these are observed frequently in class, then this may warrant further investigation.

8+ Years Old

- Still has difficulty with reading
- Reads adequately but slowly, making careless errors, and tiring in extended reading situations
- Has considerable spelling difficulties
- Good orally but written work disappointing
- Has difficulty copying accurately from the blackboard or a book
- Has failed to accumulate a core of common key words
- Still has difficulty pronouncing longer common words
- Does written work very slowly
- Misses out sounds or syllables in words, spoken and/or written
- Has difficulty memorising number bonds and tables
- Still confuses left/right and up/down
- Still has difficulty with the sequence of days, months and the alphabet
- Has poorly formed, poorly spaced immature handwriting
- Has difficulty remembering oral instructions
- Frequently appears confused and process only parts of the lesson
- Has word finding difficulties
- Poor organization and presentation; forgets books and homework
- Behaviour difficulties, frustration, poor self-image
- Easily distracted – either hyperactive or daydreaming
- Clumsy, unpopular in team games, dislikes P.E.
- Other – please give details

Screening Tools for Teachers

Many governmental and official bodies around the world are continuously publishing their approved lists of screeners that can be used by schoolteachers with the goal of providing universal screeners for students early on during their school life. For example, the Oregon Department of Education in the US produced a recent list of approved universal screening tools for risk factors of dyslexia for their 2019-2020 school year. Table 1 provides examples of screening tools both from their list and more recent ones.

As can be seen from Table 1, some of those screeners are computerized which streamlines the process and captures the screening data quickly, efficiently and

Table 1 Examples of Screening Tools for Teachers

Tool	Publisher
aimswebPlus	Pearson
DIBELS 8th Edition	Amplify Education, LLC
	University of Oregon: Center on Teaching and Learning
easyCBM	Houghton Mifflin Harcourt
	University of Oregon: Behavioural Research and Teaching
	University of Oregon: Centre on Teaching and Learning
FAST early Reading Composite + CBM reading	FastBridge Learning
EarlyBird	Earlybird Education
Star Early Literacy	Renaissance

on a mass scale. It also allows the schools to track the student's progress throughout the school year. Other such screeners include the following:

- Lucid CoPS (Cognitive Profiling System) Baseline Assessment – Singleton. (ca 4 to 5.5 years).
- Lucid CoPS (Cognitive Profiling System) – Singleton. (ca 4 to 8 years) computerized, diagnostic screening.
- LASS (Lucid Assessment Systems for Schools) Junior – Singleton. (ca 8 to 11 years) computerized multifunctional assessment.
- LASS (Lucid Assessment Systems for Schools) Secondary – Singleton. (ca 11 to 15) computerized multifunctional assessment.
- Lexia Comprehensive Reading Test (ca 5 to 18) computerized assessment.
- Lexia Quick Reading Test (ca 5 to 18) computerized assessment.
- Quickscan (third level) – computerized screening tool.
- Studyscan (third level) – computerized assessment.
- Superspell Assessment Disk (6 years to adult): Assesses user's stage of spelling development.
- Early Bird: Integrates predictive milestones with analytics to identify reading struggles before students formally learn to read.
- BrightStart: A reading readiness screener for children ages 3 to 5 years.

In addition to the above computerized screeners, there are also some screening tools that use conventional pen and paper format such as these:

- The Bangor Dyslexia Test (all ages) Miles, LDA, 1983.
- The Dyslexia Early Screening Test – 2nd ed. (ca 4.5 to 6.5) by Nicholson & Fawcett, 2003.
- The Dyslexia Screening Test (ca 6.5 to 16) by Nicholson & Fawcett, 1996.
- Group Screening Tests for Identifying Pupils at Risk with Specific Learning Disabilities (Levels Alpha; Level A; Level B; Level C; Level D;

which covers from 4.5 years of age until 16+) by Ann Arbor Publishing House, 2000.
- Slingerland High School Level Screening for the Identification of Language Strengths and Weaknesses by Murray and Beis, 1993.

There are also additional screening tools that can be used early on for children who are young learners (4 to 8 years old) such as these[3]:

- Base-line Assessment for NI. CCEA, 2000 (ca 4).
- Belfield Infant Assessment Profile (ca 4 to 7) Spelman & McHugh, Folens, 1994.
- Bury Infant Check (ca 4.1 to 5.6) Pearson & Quinn, NFER-Nelson, 1986).
- Early Literacy Test (ca 4:6 to 7:5) Hodder and Stoughton, 2000.
- Early Years Easy Screen (EYES) (ca 4 to 5). Clerehugh et al., NFER-Nelson, 1991.
- Infant Index (ca 4 to 5+) Desforges & Lindsay, Hodder & Stoughton, 1996.
- LARR[4] Test of Emergent Literacy (ca 4 to 5) NFER – Nelson, 1993.
- Middle Infants Screening Test (ca 5 to 6) Hannavy, NFER-Nelson, 1993.
- PIP Developmental Charts (ca 0 to 5) Hodder & Stoughton, 1998.
- QUEST II, Screening, Diagnostic and Remediation Kit (ca 7 to 8) Robertson et al., Arnold & Wheaton, 1995.

Error Analysis

A simple way for a teacher to begin to understand why a student is struggling with reading without having to perform the standardized tests of achievement is to conduct an error analysis of the child's work. Error analysis should be based on the elements of dyslexia as provided in the IDA's definition and summarized in the Simple View of Reading (*Decoding x Listening Comprehension = Reading Comprehension*) developed by Gough and Tunmer in 1986. For a teacher to conduct a simple error analysis in reading, the IRIS Centre at Vanderbilt University recommends the administration of a one-minute *passage reading fluency measure*. These are commonly used individually administered, timed reading passages that allows the evaluator to focus on four areas of assessment: *Reading **s**peed, **a**ccuracy, **p**rosody* (SAP) and comprehension. Many of these reading passages are available online or as part or progress monitoring instruments. Fluency is one essential component of reading and the hallmark of a good reader. The National Assessment of Educational Progress (NAEP)[5] provides a useful classification of reading fluency which we have included in Table 2.

An analysis of the type of *accuracy errors* made by the student can help teachers identify and categorize the skills of reading that are affected and in need of

Table 2 National Assessment of Educational Progress Fluency Scale

National Assessment of Educational Progress Fluency Scale			
Fluent	Level 4	Reads primarily in larger, meaningful phrase groups. Although some regressions, repetitions, and deviations from text may be present, these do not appear to detract from the overall structure of the story. Preservation of the author's syntax is consistent. Some or most of the story is read with expressive interpretation.	
Fluent	Level 3	Reads primarily in three- or four-word phrase groups. Some small groupings may be present. However, the majority of phrasing seems appropriate and preserves the syntax of the author. Little or no expressive interpretation is present.	
Non-Fluent	Level 2	Reads primarily in two-word phrases with some three- or four-word groupings. Some word-by-word reading may be present. Word groupings may seem awkward and unrelated to larger context of sentence or passage	
Non-Fluent	Level 1	Reads primarily word-by-word. Occasional two-word or three-word phrases may occur but these are infrequent and/or they do not preserve meaningful syntax.	

remediation. The IRIS Centre provides such a table online[6] that can facilitate this process. In the first column the teachers write the word that was misread and in the second column, they document the student's response. The teacher can then select the type of error from *nine error categories* provided. The categories are *sight words, beginning sounds, ending sounds, short vowels, long vowels, silent e rule, vowel teams, consonant blends and others*. Once the error pattern has been identified, the teacher can recommend further testing to obtain more information on the student's reading skills and function and begin working on remedial strategies to address the specific skills that need strengthening.

Speed can be measured by documenting the *number of words the student reads per minute*. These findings can then be compared with many of the easily accessible norm charts available online. The Hasborouck/Tindal Table (2017) is an excellent example of normed fluency charts by grade and period of the school year (e.g., Fall, Winter or Spring) and is available on multiple websites, including Reading Rockets.[7]

Prosody, the verbal expression used by the student during oral reading, is an important element of fluency. Hudson, Lane and Pullen developed a checklist to better evaluate a student's prosody.[8] Their checklist includes the following items: *Emphasis on appropriate words, tone variations at appropriate points in the text, reading inflection reflecting the punctuation and several other text boundaries and appropriate vocal tone to represent characters' mental states when reading dialogue.* This website also provides excellent teaching strategies to improve reading fluency that can be implemented in any classroom. There are several other online resources that offer useful strategies to enhance fluency skills, such as Understood.org,[9] Reading Rockets,[10] the National Centre on Improving Literacy[11] and the National Centre on Intensive Intervention.[12]

Reading comprehension can be assessed by *asking questions* about the passage the student just read. There are many standardized instruments designed to assess oral language comprehension which were described in the previous section of this chapter. Standardized vocabulary assessments have been shown to correlate well with a person's listening comprehension abilities and can be an easy way to screen for students who could be at risk for oral language challenges. One of the most common instruments is the Peabody Picture Vocabulary Test (PPVT) which has been adapted to many languages.

Progress Monitoring & RTI[13]

In the US, a three-tiered public health model have been applied to education called Response to Intervention or RTI for short. **Tier 1** refers to students identified through the universal screening who are then monitored to assess their response to instruction. **Tier 2** refers to students who are provided small group instruction and continue to be monitored to assess their response to Tier 2 intervention. **Tier 3** is provided to students who receive individual or very small group (2–3 children) instruction with a highly trained teacher. All students continue to be monitored through periodic progress monitoring assessments to ascertain their response to intervention.

As can be seen from this system, teachers should heavily rely on progress monitoring data in order to adjust their classroom instructions to meet the individual needs of their students. Progress monitoring is a form of assessment where students' learning is evaluated on a regular basis (weekly, biweekly, monthly or every three months). Such regular evaluation of students' achievement is intended to provide useful feedback about performance to both, students and their teachers. The primary purpose of progress monitoring in RTI is to determine the student's response to evidence-based instruction. As such, progress monitoring allows teachers to track students' academic progress and growth across the entire school year.

Curriculum based measurements (CBMs), which are also sometimes referred to as general outcome measurements (GOMs), are a well-known and useful form of progress monitoring because tests (referred to sometimes as *probes* or *measures*) take a few minutes to administer and score. Each measure includes sample items from every skill taught across the academic year. CBM scores tend to have high correlation to standardized tests as the scores reflect the smallest changes in student improvement. As the purpose of monitoring progress is to determine the effectiveness of an intervention plan on a student's learning, when the data shows that the students are progressing, interventions are maintained until they achieve their pre-identified goals. But, if the data shows that the students are not progressing, a change in intervention becomes necessary (Fuchs et al., 2008).[14] This would not only include making modifications to the interventional approach but also the consideration of other factors that could be impacting the student and may be preventing them from succeeding in school, such as coexisting conditions.

When students are identified as at risk for achievement deficits by universal screening measures, their progress must be then closely monitored in relation to their Tier 1 instruction. Such a progress is usually monitored at least once a month. Teachers assess and monitor their students' progress by periodically assessing their performance and comparing it with the expected rate of learning based on a local or a national benchmark. The assessment findings are then utilized by teachers to monitor the efficiency of teaching, how effective the intervention is and to adjust their teaching methods to better cater to their students' needs. Those who are not responding to Tier 1 instruction can be then moved on to Tier 2 and receive increasingly intensive intervention and instruction. Typically, teachers wait for a period of up to 8–10 weeks (McMaster & Wagner, 2007; Fuchs & Fuchs, 2005; Vaughn et al., 2003) in order to assess the effectiveness of their instruction level. Non-responsiveness is typically determined by either employing a percentile cut on norm-referenced tests or by a cut score on a CBM.[15] Effective progress-monitoring measures tend to be available in alternate forms, comparable in difficulty and conceptualization and representative of the performance desired at the end of the year (Fuchs et al., 2008). These measures should also be short and easily administered by a classroom teacher, special education teacher, or school psychologist (Fuchs & Stecker, 2003).

The RTI network provides a useful summary of the most critical reading skills to screen for in school[16] which can be summarized as follows:

- *Kindergarten skills:* Letter naming fluency, letter sound identification, blending, onset-rimes, phoneme segmentation and sound repetition.
- *1st Grade skills:* Word identification fluency, letter naming fluency, letter sound identification, phoneme segmentation, sound repetition, vocabulary and word identification fluency.
- *2nd Grade and above skills:* Oral reading fluency and comprehension-focused instruments (e.g., Scholastic Reading Inventory and 4Sight Benchmark Assessments; Slavin & Madden, 2006). These are designed to monitor progress and rescreen periodically throughout the school year.

Behavioural Observations

It is important for teachers and examiners to document observations about the student's behaviour during any testing situation or lessons in school as they will provide invaluable information regarding their state of mind at the time. These observations can also shed light into other factors that may be affecting the student's learning. Teachers can compare the student's specific behaviours when compared to their regular classmates. Below, we provide a list of some of the behaviours that are helpful to document in the classroom and during testing situations.

1. *Attention:* Is the student able to sustain attention throughout the task and block distractions?

2. *Activity level:* Is the student overactive, underactive, fidgety or too talkative?
3. *Impulsivity:* Is the student able to listen to instructions or wait for a question to be finished or being called by the teacher before providing a response. Is the student able to develop a plan for problem solving?
4. *Following and/or understanding directions:* Is the student able to follow instructions consistently? Does the student seem to understand instructions?
5. *Work habits:* Does the student seem to develop plans for problem solving and approaches testing situations and classroom projects in an organized manner? Does the student keep their workspace organized, lose school materials, complete work on time or forget to turn in completed work?
6. *Motivation:* Does the student seem engaged with the task and put forth appropriate effort?
7. *Anxiety:* Does the student demonstrate excessive worry or concern about their performance, making mistakes or other factors? Does the student seem withdrawn or exceedingly timid? Does the child complain of frequent headaches or other body aches, not feeling well or feeling tired?
8. *Depression:* Does the student seem very sad? Does the child seem to have lost interest in activities that they used to enjoy, has lost their spark and/or lacks enjoyment of life?
9. *Mood/feelings:* Does the student present as particularly irritable or with very flat affect/mood? Is the child defiant, argumentative or aggressive?

Notes

1. Presentation for the Reading League of Florida by Stephanie Hammerschmidt-Sidarich, PhD (August 2021) Being Intentional: Selecting Efficient, and Effective Instructional Practices that Align with Student Needs.
2. This section is taken with permission from The Dyslexia Assessment (2018) by Gavin Reid and Jennie Guise, Bloomsbury, UK.
3. www.sess.ie/dyslexia-section/lists-tests Dated 21st July 2021.
4. Linguistic Awareness in Reading Readiness.
5. https://nces.ed.gov/pubs95/web/95762.asp
6. https://iris.peabody.vanderbilt.edu/module/dbi2/cresource/q2/p06/
7. www.readingrockets.org/sites/default/files/2017%20ORF%20NORMS.pdf
8. www.readingrockets.org/article/understanding-and-assessing-fluency
9. www.understood.org/articles/en/improve-reading-fluency-children
10. www.readingrockets.org/article/developing-fluent-readers
11. https://improvingliteracy.org/brief/four-steps-building-fluency-text
12. https://intensiveintervention.org/
13. https://iris.peabody.vanderbilt.edu/module/rti-math/cresource/q1/p05/ Retrieved July 22, 2021.
14. www.branchingminds.com/what-does-progress-monitoring-look-like-in-response-to-intervention
15. Further information can be obtained from: www.rtinetwork.org/learn/research/progress-monitoring-within-a-rti-model
16. www.rtinetwork.org/essential/assessment/screening/readingproblems

5 Evaluate

Understanding a Psychoeducational Evaluation Report

Test Types

A comprehensive evaluation should include all the *LEFT* four elements described in Chapter 2. In this chapter we will focus on the standardized tests that typically are administered as part of a comprehensive evaluation. Which tests are administered will depend on the type of assessment being conducted. As described in Chapter 1 there are many different types of comprehensive evaluations (psychoeducational, psychological, neuropsychological and multidisciplinary) performed by many different professionals. However, they all have several factors in common. There is usually an assessment of the student's cognitive abilities, often in the form of an IQ or cognitive tests, tests of cognitive processing, tests of achievement and standardized behavioural scales. These instruments measure the student's mental age or cognitive level, their learning profile and processing abilities, academic achievement and behaviour and emotional profile. This bird's eye view can help you understand the multiple factors that are impacting the student's quality of life as described in the Rule of Fours (work performance, behaviour/emotional regulation, social interaction and health).

As previously noted, *cognitive and processing tests* evaluate neurodevelopmental functions that impact the acquisition of reading, writing and mathematics abilities. Some of the most commonly used cognitive instruments are the Weschler Scales (WPPSI, WISC, WAIS), the Stanford Binet Intelligence Scales and the Woodcock-Johnson Test of Cognitive Abilities (WJ-C). Other tests include the Reynolds Intellectual Assessment Scales (RIAS), the Differential Ability Scales (DAS), and the Universal Nonverbal Intelligence Test (UNIT). There are several other tests in this category, but we will primarily focus on the WISC as it is a very commonly used instrument. Many of the processing functions assessed are included in many of the IQ, cognitive and achievement tests and in other instruments that are specific to particular processing skills, such as phonological processing, oral language skills, visual perceptual and motor abilities, working memory and rapid automatized naming. Please refer to Chapter 8 where we provide lists of these tests and the functions that they assess.

Tests of achievement are designed to quantify the student's level of performance in the basic skills and their application in reading, writing and arithmetic abilities. As such, most tests of reading achievement will include assessment of word attack skills (single word decoding and fluency) and reading comprehension. Many of the most recent versions of these tests will also assess some of the basic functions necessary for reading including phonological processing, working memory and rapid automatized naming.

Finally, *Global Behavioural Scales* offer a quantification of the student's behaviours by categorizing them into internalizing, externalizing and atypical behaviour patterns. These types of instruments offer reports based on clinical scales that include behaviours like aggression, conduct problems, attention, hyperactivity, anxiety, depression, somatization, withdrawal and learning problems. The most commonly used global behaviour scales in the US, the Behaviour Assessment System for Children (BASC) and the Achenbach System of Empirically Based Assessment (ASEBA), categorize behaviours into internalizing, externalizing and atypical patterns. They offer parent, teacher and student forms and generate easy to interpret reports. An advantage of these Global Behaviour Scales is that they have been translated and adapted to multiple languages and cultures. On many occasions, the evaluation report may include disorder specific scales for assessment of different disorders, such as ADHD, anxiety, depression, oppositional/conduct and autism spectrum disorders.

So, you observed the student, communicated with the parents and, following your advice, a psychoeducational evaluation was performed. The parents have shared the report with you and want your opinion and plan for helping their child. You look at the report and feel a bit overwhelmed and maybe even intimidated by it. No worries, we will walk you through the steps to get as much information as you can from it in a simple, no-nonsense manner. An important concept to remember is that the tests are intended to quantify the strengths and weaknesses of the student. It should not tell you anything that you don't already know.

Step 1: Ascertain the Type of Evaluation

What you want to know:

- What type of assessment was performed?

Why you want to know it:

- The purpose of these evaluations is different.
    - Psychoeducational = **Eligibility for services**
    - Psychological = **Diagnosis**
    - Neuropsychological = **Causes**
    - Multidisciplinary = **Cause, diagnosis(es) & eligibility data**

In Chapter 1, we described the different types of dyslexia assessments and the professionals that administer them. If the evaluation was performed by the school, it is likely that the purpose of the assessment was to ascertain eligibility for services. An evaluation performed by a psychologist, neuropsychologist or multidisciplinary team outside of the school system will most likely focus on making a diagnosis, identifying the factors contributing to the clinical presentation and offering some recommendations to address the identified challenges.

Step 2: Was the Assessment Performed Following Best Practices?

The simplest way to determine this is to see if the assessment included the four components of *LEFT* described in Chapter 2. That is:

- *L – Listen:* Did the evaluator document a comprehensive history including early markers of dyslexia and educational history, family history of learning difficulties, a history of possible coexisting conditions and a general medical history? (Please refer to Chapter 2 for more details on a proper history.)
- *E – Evaluate:* Did the report provide the results of standardized assessments that focus on the essential elements to assess dyslexia? That is, the examiner(s) ought to document the tests administered at the beginning of the report. In this chapter we will emphasize the instruments and their specific applications in the assessment of a student suspected of having dyslexia. These tests include the following:
    - *Overall level of developmental functioning and cognitive processes* (IQ and cognitive processing tests): the definition of dyslexia states that the problems are not due to lack of intelligence. Therefore, you want to have a good understanding of the student's level of developmental functioning as this should be consistent with the student's level of academic performance.
    - *Academic achievement skills*: These tests will evaluate the skills and neurodevelopmental functions needed for reading. Therefore, an appropriate assessment must document the basic elements of reading, *word attack skills and language comprehension*, as described in IDA's definition of dyslexia discussed in Chapter 1. As such, we should expect that if a student has dyslexia the evaluation will reveal good oral language comprehension abilities but weak word attack skills. Word attack skills testing must include phonic decoding and fluency while the assessment of reading comprehension should incorporate an evaluation of overall language skills, background knowledge and executive functions. These skills and functions must be adequately assessed in order to make an appropriate diagnosis of dyslexia.

        When reporting on cognitive and achievement tests, the examiner will usually provide a description of how each skill is measured. This is important information because a particular skill may be measured in a way that is different from how the student applies that skill in school.

For example, a child who struggles with reading in school may attain a very high score on a reading comprehension test administered during the psychoeducational evaluation which is inconsistent with their performance in the classroom. While at first glance, this does not seem to make sense, when you read the test description it explains that they used a cloze procedure (fill in the blanks) to assess this skill. However, in the classroom you have been evaluating reading comprehension by asking open ended questions. Because the student is quite smart and is often able to figure out the answer in a fill-in-the-blanks or multiple-choice test, despite weak word attack skills, this may explain the difference between the test and classroom performance.

- *Assessment of behaviour and emotional conditions*: This is an especially important component of the assessment evaluation process. Psychologists usually accomplish this in two ways: Documenting their behavioural observations and administering standardized behaviour scales. Behavioural Observations is a section of the report that usually precedes the actual test results. This is expected to include a description of the student's behaviour during testing. These observations are particularly important because they offer insight into the students' mindset during the testing, which may have a significant impact on their performance. Some of these observations may include inattention, anxiety, fatigue, or poor motivation or engagement. For example, if the child was not appropriately engaged during the evaluation, the findings may not be valid. In addition, the behavioural observations often include information about the state of mind or *mental status* of the individual, including appearance and orientation in time (date and time of day), space (where they are located, their home address, etc.) and person (knowing their name, age, etc.), their mood and overall behavioural and emotional demeanour. Chapter 4 provides a summary of the type of documentation that should be included in the behavioural observations. Below, we provide a case sample where the evaluator offered an excellent summary of a child's behaviour during the assessment:

Richard was evaluated over the course of one session lasting approximately 4.5 hours with many breaks throughout. He presented as a polite, friendly and outgoing child. He was easily engaged in conversation and rapport was easily established as he discussed his interests. Richard reported a variety of age-appropriate interests and exhibited a typically developing or better level of interpersonal communication and expressive language skills.

What do these behavioural observations tell us about Richard during the testing situation?
- They indicate that the findings are likely valid because he was engaged and cooperative during the testing.
- It makes a point of describing strong oral language skills, so it eliminates a more global language disorder as a potential factor in Richard's challenges.

Richard was compliant and responded well to simple verbal redirection throughout the evaluation session. He very frequently tended to engage in "stream of consciousness" verbal tangents in the middle of evaluation tasks. While the frequency of these verbal tangents was high, it was evident that he was not doing it to avoid or escape tasks he found difficult or aversive. These difficulties with self-regulation are considered symptoms of his ADHD rather than purposeful or willful behaviours toward some end goal. He responded well to a non-verbal gesture that simply informed him that he was becoming off task. He did not exhibit any hyperactivity or behavioural impulsivity. He did not answer questions in an impulsive manner and appeared to take his time on tasks that were challenging. He persevered through tasks that were difficult and those that required sustained mental effort. No outward signs of anxiety were noted. Richard did engage in helpful self-talk strategies such as telling himself "it's ok if you get a question wrong. It's no big deal and you just might need more practice!". Overall, Richard put forth his best effort and these results appear to be valid estimates of his academic achievement and intellectual functioning".

What do these behavioural observations tell us about Richard during the testing situation?
- There is an indication of attention problems during the testing.
- The examiner also pointed out strategies that helped Richard's attention problems (e.g., non-verbal redirection) which could be useful in school.
- There was no indication of oppositional or significant anxiety symptoms. He used positive self talk to continue to maintain effort throughout difficult sections of the testing. another strategy that can be useful at school.

Behavioural observations should be thought of as a "snapshot" in time. The behaviour of examinees during the evaluation may not be representative of their larger patterns of behaviour at home and in school. The evaluation environment tends to differ from home and school in several key ways that may change a child's behaviour. The evaluation environment and evaluator are often novel for an examinee. If a child is unsure about their environment, the expectations of the tasks or the evaluator, they may exert a greater level of physical and mental self-control or they may exhibit behaviour that "tests limits". Thus, a child may exhibit a greater or lesser degree of impairment in terms of any emotional control, impulsivity, hyperactivity and attention regulation. The behaviours described in this portion of the report should be thought of as a "snapshot" in time as opposed to a representative sample.

What does this comment by the examiner tell us about behavioural observations during testing?

- It cautions readers that the behaviours described above may not represent what they usually observe at school or at home because testing is a very unique setting.

What this sample of behavioural observations provides is not only a description of the observed behaviours but a clear explanation of the differences between a natural setting, such as home and school and a testing situation.

A second component of the assessment of the student's behaviour and emotional status is the use of standardized behaviour questionnaires. These can be general in nature or disorder specific. For example, the BASC and ASEBA are general behaviour questionnaires that screen for the presence of internalizing, externalizing and atypical disorders. On the other hand, behaviour questionnaires, such as the Conners, Vanderbilt, Screen for Child Anxiety Related Disorders (SCARED), Colombia DISC Depression Scale, and many others are designed to screen or diagnose specific disorders.

- *F – Formulate:* This is probably the most important section of the report because it should provide an explanation for the student's challenges, not only as it pertains to reading, but to any of the other aspects of the child's life that may be impacting learning. In general terms, the formulation should provide a description of the following areas:
  - Diagnosis(es)
  - Level of functioning
  - Achievement and processing
  - Attention related issues
  - Behavioural/Emotional concerns
  - Social interaction skills
  - Health factors
  - Social/Environmental factors

  In this section of the report the examiner should provide a clear explanation and rationale for the diagnosis and test interpretation. A good description of the strengths and weaknesses of the student should lead to a good prescription for management. This will be further discussed in Chapter 6.
- *T – Teach/Treat:* Finally, the report should provide suggestions on how to address the challenges identified by the evaluation (history and test results). This should include recommendations for academic remediation, modifications and accommodations strategies that can help the student. If appropriate, the report should provide enough data to help the school system ascertain eligibility criteria for services. It is important to understand that eligibility is a fiscal/administrative decision, independent of the student needs. The evaluation should always provide recommendations to address the student's needs documented in the report. These may include psychological and medical interventions. Chapter 7 provides more details in this regard.

Interpreting Test Results

Step 3: Let's do the numbers! Interpreting the test results can, at first, seem like a daunting task. Looking at the scores can be confusing because often times the test scores are reported in different units of measurements. The important thing to remember is that regardless of the type of score, the scores all represent the same value in different ways. For example, let's say that you want to buy an item online from another country, but you are not familiar with their currency. In order to figure out the cost, you have to convert it to the currency of your country. The value of the item does not change, but the price number will change based on the currency (e.g., dollars, pound sterling, Euro, etc.). So, if you are familiar with one particular currency, all you have to do is use a currency converter and you know exactly how much it will cost, whether it is a reasonable price, and if it is consistent with what you expected.

In the case of test scores, the units of measurement may vary, even within a test. Some of the "currencies" of psychological test are standard scores. Others

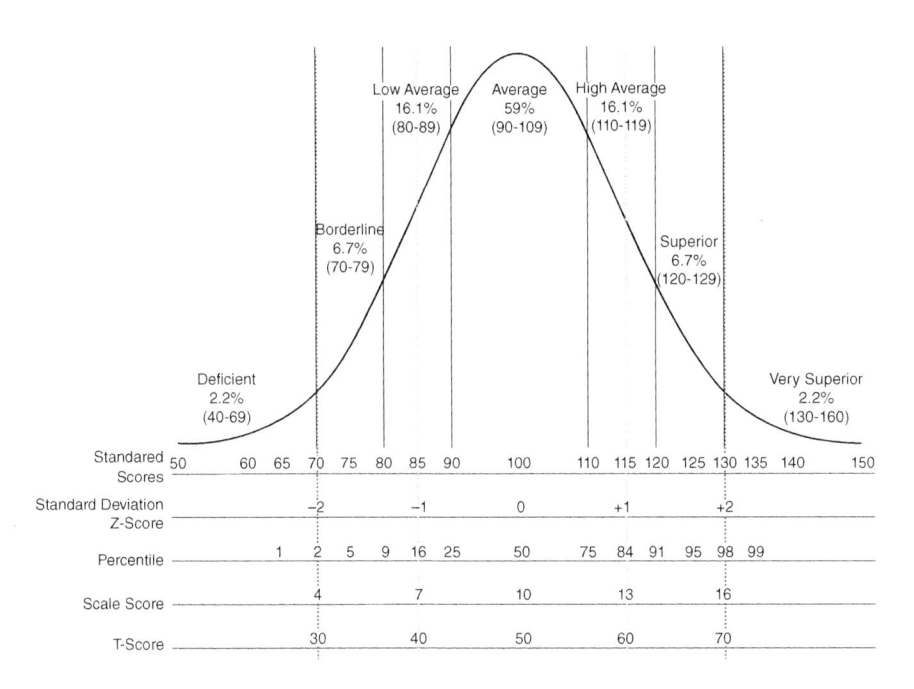

Figure 3 The bell-shaped curve in this figure can serve as your currency converter. As you can see, there are several different units of measurement or "currencies" listed on the lower left column of the curve. The value of each "currency" (e.g., standard scores, standard deviations, percentiles, scaled scores and T-scores) is provided on each row next to the units of measurement. Using this approach, one can easily see that a standard score of 85 is the same as 1 standard deviation below the mean, a performance in the 16th percentile, a Scaled Score of 7 or a T-Score of 40. This will help you choose the "currency" that makes the most sense to you. The qualitative descriptors above the top of each column (e.g., Average, Low Average, High Average, etc.) can be an indicator of the possible impact on Richard's classroom performance in comparison to other students.

include scaled scores, percentiles, and T-scores. When we were evaluating students in the early stages of our careers, we found this confusing until we rediscovered a clever "currency converter" for psychoeducational test results: The **bell-shaped curve**. This is represented in Figure 3. The diagram shows different units of measurement or "currency" on the left (e.g., Standard Scores, Z-Score, Percentile, Scaled Score, T-Score) while the interpretation or qualitative descriptors of the scores are provided above the curve (e.g., Deficient, Borderline, Low-Average, Average, High-Average, Superior, Very Superior). Following the currency analogy, qualitative descriptors would indicate the relative cost of the item (e.g., Extremely Inexpensive, Very Inexpensive, Inexpensive, Average Cost, Expensive, Very Expensive, Extremely Expensive).

So, like in the example of different currencies, if I get a report of a student's performance reported as a Standard Score of 100, but I am only familiar with percentiles, by looking at the diagram, I can tell that this child is performing in the 50th percentile, or the average range.

Another critical factor to consider when looking at the numbers is the pattern of distribution of the scores. This is where you may find the explanation to the student's reading challenges. We will use the example below to explain this in more detail.

> *L – Listen:* Richard is a seven-year-old boy entering second grade who presents with a history of reading, writing and math difficulties since he started school. His early history revealed articulation difficulties which resulted in poor intelligibility of speech. At school, he struggles with rhyming, letter recognition and letter-sound correspondence. His hearing and vision were reported to be normal. Richard was recently diagnosed as having ADHD and is being treated with medication, but his reading and spelling difficulties persist. There is a strong family history of learning and attention problems.

E – Evaluate: Test results are listed in Table 3.

Cognitive/Developmental Functioning **WISC-V**

Table 3 Examples of Test Results

Scale	Composite Score	Percentile Rank
Verbal Comprehension	111	77
Visual–Spatial	100	50
Fluid Reasoning	94	34
Working Memory	79	8
Processing Speed	83	13
Full Scale IQ	94	34

Psychoeducational Evaluation Report 45

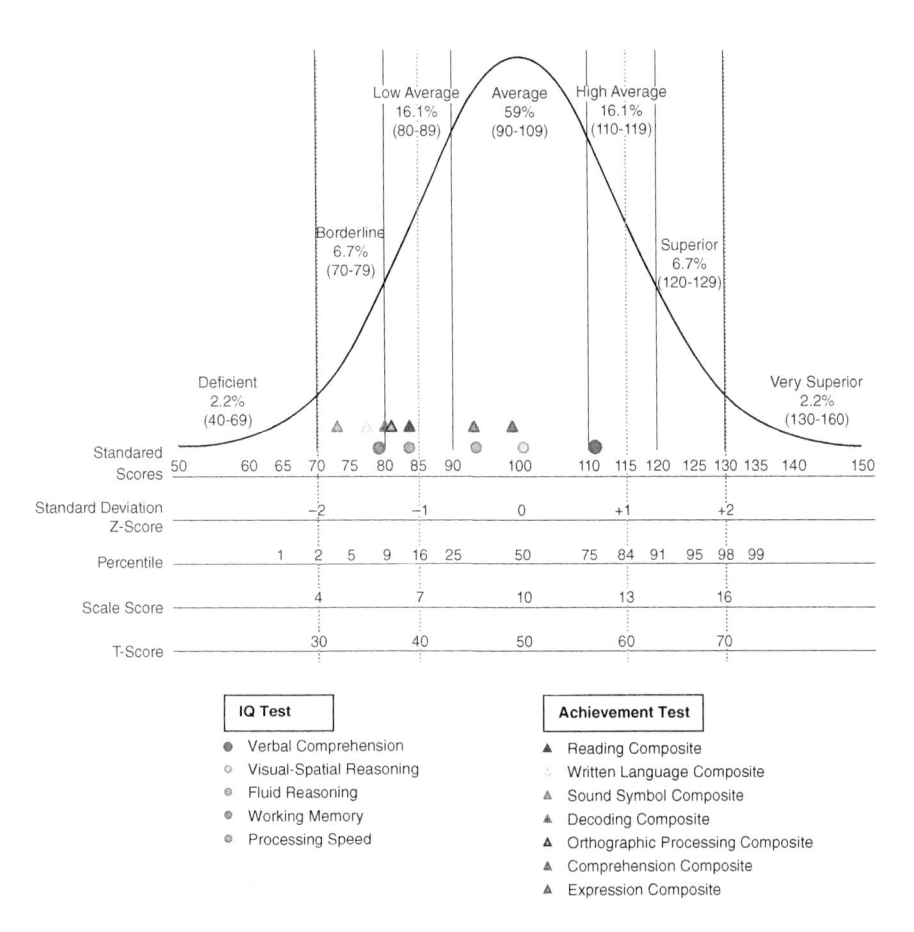

Figure 4 Test results example

Clearly, Richard's scores do not fall in a tight cluster as it would be expected. The numbers indicate is that his verbal reasoning scores fall in the high average range, while his working memory scores are in the borderline range. This represents a huge difference indicating definitive strengths in verbal comprehension (77th percentile) but weak working memory (8th percentile). The other scores are relatively close to one another, with the exception of processing speed (13th percentile). These differences may be related to Richard's diagnosis of dyslexia and ADHD.

Richard was also administered the Kaufman Test of Educational Achievement, 3rd Edition (KTEA-3) which evaluated academic skills, phonological processing, orthographic processing and academic language development. The results are listed in Table 4.

Table 4 Example Results

Core Composites & Subtests	Age-Based Standard Score	Percentile Rank
Letter & Word Recognition	84	14
Reading Comprehension	87	19
Reading Composite	**84**	**14**
Written Expression	77	6
Spelling	77	6
Written Language Composite	**77**	**6**
Phonological Processing	78	7
Nonsense Word Decoding	78	7
Sound-Symbol Composite	**74**	**4**
Letter & Word Recognition	84	14
Nonsense Word Decoding	78	7
Decoding Composite	**80**	**9**
Spelling	77	6
Letter Naming Facility	95	37
Word Recognition Facility	82	12
Orthographic Processing Composite	**81**	**10**
Reading Comprehension	87	19
Listening Comprehension	111	77
Comprehension Composite	**99**	**47**
Written Expression	77	6
Oral Expression	114	82
Expression Composite	**94**	**34**

By studying the pattern of the scores, you can quickly recognize the challenges that the student has. Furthermore, these findings are consistent with the history. They simply quantified the problem. One of the more striking findings of the KTEA-3 is the significant strengths Richard demonstrated in Listening Comprehension and Oral Expression. These results are also consistent with the Verbal Comprehension scores on the WISC-V. What this tells us is that Richard's language comprehension skills are within the High Average Range while his reading and writing skills fall most consistently within the Low Average to Borderline Range. These test results are consistent with a classic clinical picture of a student with dyslexia. That is, this is a child who has strong oral language skills, yet his reading comprehension and written expression are significantly below expectation as a result of deficits in phonological processing.

In the next two chapters we will discuss the formulation and how to Teach & Treat.

6 Formulation

Putting It All Together

As previously described in Chapter 2, every dyslexia assessment should provide answers to five questions.

1. *Does the student have a significant challenge/is there really a problem?*
2. *What is it called (diagnosis -es)?*
3. *What is (are) the cause(s)?*
4. *What can be done?*
5. *What can be expected in the future?*

The **Formulation** is the section in the report where these questions should be answered. As indicated in the previous chapter, this is a critical step in the evaluation process because it integrates the history (**L**istening), with teacher, student and parents' observations and test results (**E**valuate – Standardized tests end error analysis). The *Formulation* provides the foundation for how to **T**each and **T**reat the student. This section of a report can also be referred to as "Assessment" or "Summary of Findings". It should include a description of the problems, their severity, lists of the diagnoses (when appropriate) along with the interpretation of the history and test results which describe the causes or contributing factors to the student's impairment. These findings should identify the different functions and skills that will require intervention and the strengths that can help the student overcome them. In other words, this is where the justification for specific interventions is provided as supported by the evidence documented by the history and testing. Similarly, the formulation should provide sufficient documentation for the appropriate agencies to ascertain if the student is eligible for special education services and/or accommodations or modifications at school. At the same time, the Formulation should identify areas of strength that can help the student succeed in life.

In this chapter we will focus on the first three questions listed above. Chapter 7 will address management (What can be done?). The last question, "What can be expected in the future?", is something that should be addressed by each of the professionals performing the assessment rather than the teacher. In order to answer the questions pertinent to this chapter, we propose that the findings of the evaluation should be presented following the Rule of Fours discussed in Chapter 2.

DOI: 10.4324/9781003212058-6

Formulation Structure – The Rule of Fours

As you may recall, the Rule of Fours suggests that if you have a description of how the four major contributing factors (developmental profile, behavioural and emotional profile, health and environmental factors) affect the student's quality of life by causing impairment, you will have a good idea of the type of interventions needed. The four areas of impairment are these: Academic performance, behaviour and emotional regulation, social relationships and health. In other words, the evaluation should strive to provide a good description of how the contributing factors impact the student's quality of life which should lead to a good prescription in any of the four main areas of intervention: Educational, psychological, medical and environmental intervention. Let us now look at these major contributing factors in more detail.

Cognitive & Processing Skills

This section should combine the qualitative and quantitative data. The qualitative data consists of the descriptions of the student's academic skills provided by the parents, the teachers and the student. Quantitative data includes the results of progress monitoring and error analysis as well as the standardized tests findings administered. These data should give sufficient information to ascertain if the child meets diagnostic criteria for a diagnosis of dyslexia and other related disorders and provide enough documentation to formulate an appropriate plan of intervention. Based on the IDA's definition of dyslexia and the Simple View of Reading, the formulation should provide data related to the functions and skills associated with them. We can separate these into the cognitive functions that impact reading and the actual reading skills.

Since all learning disorders are by definition unexpected there should be a general estimation of the child's overall cognitive development or mental age to ensure that the cause of the learning challenges is not the result of a more global developmental disorder, such as an intellectual disability. While this may be inferred from the history, an IQ test can provide a more objective idea of the student's overall level of cognitive development. A verbal IQ can offer a description of the student's vocabulary level and verbal reasoning skills. In addition, some IQ and cognitive abilities tests can provide an indication of the student's general fund of knowledge. Other critical skills assessed by these tests include working memory, processing speed, visual spatial reasoning and fluid reasoning.

Phonological processing and rapid naming will impact single word decoding. Most academic achievement tests can provide a good indication of the student's phonic decoding and fluency skills. These tests should provide sufficient information of the child's performance on word identification, word recognition and spelling. These learned skills are dependent on cognitive processes and acquired skills such as phonological skills, rapid naming, orthographic knowledge and vocabulary abilities. It is important to understand how each skill is measured in order to properly interpret the findings.

- *Phonic decoding:* Tests that evaluate phonological processing usually focus on these skills. This is a critical element of the dyslexia assessment, especially those tasks that evaluate phonemic awareness. The evaluation of dyslexia should include tests that assess the identification and manipulation (deletion, substitution and blending) of individual sounds and syllables. While there are tests specifically designed to evaluate phonological processing, some achievement tests also provide excellent assessments of these functions. We provide a list of these instruments in Chapter 8.
- *Sight word memory:* Tests that measure these skills emphasize orthographic knowledge and long-term phonological memory. In order to do this the student must recognize the sequence of letters as representing a particular sequence of sounds (orthographic knowledge) which has a specific meaning (semantics) stored in long-term memory. These are essential factors that impact fluency. Rapid naming is a component of sight word memory. So, when you are looking at test results find subtests that include terms like rapid (digit, letter, picture or colour) naming. Some of the tests that assess these skills include the Test of Word Reading Efficiency (TOWRE), Word Reading (WIAT-III) and Digit & Picture Span (WISC-V, Woodcock Johnson).

Academic Achievement

Receptive and expressive oral language abilities are an essential component of reading and writing skills. After all, they are language arts subjects! As such, some of the standardized academic achievement tests used in the assessment should document the student's general language comprehension skills. Some of these language elements include vocabulary (word breadth and depth), language structures (syntax – sentence structure and semantics – at the word, phrase, sentence and discourse level), verbal reasoning (metaphors, inference making, problem solving) and literacy knowledge (text structure and genre). Speech language evaluations provide the most detailed language assessments. However, some of these elements are evaluated in other types of tests such as IQ and processing tests. Other functions that will impact language comprehension include attention, monitoring and working memory.

In addition to measuring the functions that impact reading (phonic decoding and sight word memory), academic achievement tests measure the student's overall performance in these acquired skills. Achievement tests can measure fluency through oral reading by evaluating not only the student's speed and accuracy when reading single words but also by assessing the prosody or intonation when reading a passage. Furthermore, you can gain a great deal of information on phonological processing from the results of spelling tests as they require orthographic mapping (speech to print activities) which is dependent on phonological processing. Similarly, written expression tests can provide an indication of the student's executive functions, topic and background knowledge, genre and text structure conventions and expressive language skills as writing requires organization, planning and the incorporation of multiple subskills in order to a generate meaningful content. Arithmetic assessment, particularly problem solving, or math application testing can also provide insight into reading challenges. A child with good computational skills who struggles with word problems in math may be experiencing reading problems rather than a math learning disorder. Research has also demonstrated that persons diagnosed with dyslexia have a greater likelihood of experiencing numerosity (number sense) challenges.

The above descriptions are applicable to English speaking students. There are many other factors that must be considered when evaluating English language learners, such as the language spoken at home, the language of instruction, and their proficiency in English oral language skills, to name a few.

Attention & Executive Functions

Attention is an essential function that will affect every aspect of reading. It is also one of the symptoms required for the diagnosis of an ADHD, one of the most common coexisting conditions associated with dyslexia. The most appropriate way to make this diagnosis is by obtaining a thorough history and quantifying the findings with standardized questionnaires. It is most important to remember that the questionnaires must document sufficient symptoms (six or more under the age of 17 years) of inattention and/or hyperactivity/impulsivity in more than one environment (typically home and school), for a duration no less than six months. In addition, the symptoms must cause impairment. The impairment associated with ADHD includes decreased productivity and accuracy of schoolwork (not due to a skill deficit like dyslexia, but as a result of inattention, poor planning and impulsivity), increased disruptive behaviour and/or non-compliance, lack of social awareness and increased health risks. Some of the most common instruments used to diagnosed ADHD include the Vanderbilt Scales, The Conners Scales and The Brown Scales.

Behavioural & Emotional Factors

During this section of the formulation, it is important to document any significant internalizing, externalizing or atypical behaviour patterns identified by the history and/or through the administration of standardized behaviour questionnaires. Behavioural and emotional symptoms can have a dramatic impact on learning. There are two types of behaviour questionnaires that are used in the diagnosis of behavioural and emotional disorders. These include general behaviour questionnaires/scales and those that are disorder specific/scales.

Many of these instruments include parent, teacher and student forms and have been adapted to multiple languages. The most commonly used general behaviour scales are the Child Behaviour Checklist (CBCL) and the Behaviour Assessment System for Children (BASC).

There are many disorder specific instruments available which focus on particular diagnoses: For example, the previously mentioned ADHD-related scales. There are also many anxiety, depression and autism spectrum disorder scales.

As noted earlier, human behaviours are classified in three major patterns: *Internalizing, Externalizing and Atypical Disorders.*

Internalizing Disorders: Children who experience these disorders tend to "keep things in". In other words, they internalize their emotions which makes them, at times, difficult to recognize. For example, a child who shuts down in school may be suffering from an anxiety disorder that is likely coexisting, aggravated, or the result of dyslexia. Internalizing disorders may also result in test anxiety, irritability and/or social withdrawal. This section of the formulation should describe the behavioural and emotional symptoms, possible diagnoses and the effect that these may have in the student's day-to-day performance in the specific domains of impairment.

Externalizing Disorders: As the word implies, children who are diagnosed with externalizing disorders tend to "act out" their symptoms. As a result, they are very easy to identify because they tend to cause a great deal of disruption in the classroom. As expected, these types of behaviour patterns can hinder learning in a significant way. A child who reacts in an oppositional and/or defiant way when asked to read may be reacting this way to cover up a reading difficulty. In our practice we have interviewed many children who indicated that they would rather be perceived as being "bad" rather than "dumb". As with internalizing disorders, the formulation should identify the symptoms, the impact they have on the student's performance and the diagnosis. Most of the general behaviour scales and some of the ADHD rating scales include externalizing symptoms associated with oppositional defiant and conduct disorders.

Atypical Disorders: Students with these types of challenges, such as an ASD, may experience significant difficulties with behaviour and, possibly, reading comprehension. Inflexible or stereotypical thinking often results in trouble adjusting to changes and transitions which may lead to behaviour outbursts in children experiencing these challenges. One of the main factors that defines ASD is the significant difficulty that many of them experience with pragmatic language skills. These include the interpretation of nonverbal communication skills, such as eye contact, facial expressions, body language and the use of idiomatic expressions. This last factor can impact the interpretation of figurative language in written work as well as inference and extrapolation in oral and written language. Several of the general behaviour scales provide questions to evaluate atypical disorders. There are also many disorder-specific scales for the diagnosis of autism spectrum disorders.

Health & Family Medical History Factors

Since health factors can impact learning, it is important to document if there are any. A good comprehensive evaluation should document the presence of any significant health disorder. For example, students who have chronic illnesses may require hospital or homebound instruction and may miss critical educational experiences. As previously mentioned, sleep factors can have a major impact on alertness, attention, endurance and learning. Furthermore, it is also important to document if a student is taking medications as some of them may have an effect on mood, attention, alertness or other factors that will impact learning. This information should be shared by the parents with the prescribing physician as it may lead to a change in the student's medical treatment. Finally, family health history is another important component of an evaluation as many of these conditions are hereditary. Thus, it is important to document if there is a family history of dyslexia and coexisting disorders.

Social/Environmental Factors

Given the impact that stress factors at home or school can have on a student's performance, it is important to document those. For example, a student who recently moved in from another country may experience multiple challenges associated with such a big transition. Changes in family structure, health or finances can also impact a child's learning. Social competency is an excellent predictor of good outcomes in life. Therefore, it is important to describe the individual's ability to relate to others, including level of comfort with peers, sportsmanship, empathy, reciprocity, manners, etc. Similarly, the peer group can have a very significant impact on the student's performance in school, particularly during the middle and high school years and as such, any assessment of learning disorders should include a description of the student's social skills.

If we consider the case of our sample student, Richard, we can combine the findings of the history with those of the evaluation to give us a clear picture of all of the factors that are impacting Richard's learning. His Formulation could read as follows:

- *Developmental Profile: Richard presents with* **average developmental functioning** *(WISC-V FSIQ 34th percentile) and* **high average Listening Comprehension abilities** *(WISC-V Verbal Comprehension, K-TEA Listening Comprehension 77th percentile).* **Average Visual Spatial abilities** *(50th percentile) and* **Fluid Reasoning** *(34th percentile) were also documented by the WISC. Richard experienced* **difficulties with Working Memory** *(8th percentile) and* **Processing speed** *(13th percentile). Weaknesses in working memory can impact decoding, reading comprehension, written language and math problem solving. Delays in processing speed can affect fluency.*

The results of the evaluation also revealed **significant deficits in basic reading skills** such as **word decoding accuracy** *(KTEA-3 Letter & Word Recognition – 14th percentile, Nonsense Word Decoding – 7th percentile),* **word reading fluency** *(Word Recognition Fluency – 12th percentile)* **phonological awareness** *(CTOPP-2 Phonological Awareness composite – 12th percentile, KTEA-3 Phonological Processing – 7th percentile),* and **phonological working memory** *(WISC-V WMI – 8th percentile, CTOPP-2 Phonological Memory composite – 3rd percentile). Each of these areas are measures of key reading related skills that closely predict future reading achievement and explain the nature of Richard's difficulties in reading. These difficulties are unexpected given that his level of general cognitive functioning falls in the Average Range (WISC-V Full Scale IQ – 34th percentile) and his verbal language skills are above average (WISC-V Verbal Comprehension Index – 77th percentile). This contrasts with his performance on Reading Comprehension which fell at the 19th percentile. It is clear that Richard's reading comprehension difficulties are the result of word level reaching challenges.*

Richard's evaluation results, when interpreted in conjunction with the fact that he is receiving regular supplemental intervention and with symptoms that have been present since preschool will meet criteria for **Specific Learning Disorder with Impairment in Reading (DSM-5 315.00, ICD-10 F81.9) based on a lack of word reading accuracy and fluency, also known as dyslexia.**

The very large discrepancy between Richard's oral expression (KTEA-3 Oral Expression – 82nd percentile) and his written expression (KTEA-3 Written Expression – 6th percentile) indicates that he is able to communicate quite well verbally and that his difficulties are isolated to the written modality. Similarly, his challenges in phonological processing are impacting his spelling skills (KTEA-3 Spelling – 6th percentile). His performance on this evaluation will also meet criteria for **Specific Learning Disorder with Impairment in Written Expression (DSM-5 315.2, ICD-10 F81.81) based on deficits in spelling accuracy, grammar and clarity of written expression.**

Richard also demonstrates difficulty with inattention at home and at school in spite of currently taking stimulant medication. Impulsivity and hyperactivity do not appear to be a major factor impacting his performance since stimulant medication was prescribed. His performance on the ADHD rating scale meets diagnostic criteria for an **attention deficit hyperactivity disorder, predominantly inattentive presentation (ICD-10 F90.0).** *The change in presentation from combined to inattentive is likely the result of his current medical treatment. That is, his dose of medication may be sufficient to address hyperactivity and impulsivity symptoms but not those of inattention.*

This section of the Formulation explicitly lists the cognitive components that impact learning, the achievement level in basic academic skills and a clear description of why the student is struggling with reading and writing. Furthermore, it documented the significant impact that Richard's attention problems are having in his learning.

- *Behaviour Profile: Richard is demonstrating symptoms suggesting an internalizing disorder. His mother describes him as experiencing excessive worrying, restlessness, irritability and muscle tension while his teachers report that he is easily overwhelmed. His performance on the SCARED revealed clinically significant scores on the* **Generalized Anxiety Disorder subscale.** *While Richard is also displaying some defiant and oppositional symptoms these behaviours appear to be triggered by anxiety provoking situations and are limited to the home environment.* **These findings are consistent with a diagnosis of a generalized anxiety disorder (ICD-10 F41.1).**

- *Peer Interactions/Social Skills: Richard is reported to interact better with younger children. He tends to be somewhat withdrawn with same age peers which has resulted in diminished social interaction at school as he struggles to make friends. This may be a result of his anxiety symptoms.*

  This section of the Formulation describes the impact that Richard's anxiety symptoms may be having on his social interaction.

- *Medical Factors: There are no reports of any significant medical problems impacting Richard's academic performance.*

  The absence of medical and environmental factors (described in the section below) should be documented to ensure the reader of the report that these aspects of the child's life have been included as part of the assessment.

- *Social/Environmental: There are no reports of any major environmental factors, other than his inability to meet academic expectations in reading and writing for his grade.*

The Formulation in the case sample above answers the first three questions described at the beginning of this chapter. It demonstrates that there is a problem with reading and writing that is quite significant as quantified by scores on standardized tests. The findings confirm his reported difficulties with reading and writing and describe in detail the contributing factors or causes to these academic challenges. Richard's deficits in phonemic awareness, his inattention and anxiety as well as his difficulties with working memory and processing speed explain why he is struggling academically, emotionally and socially. In addition, the summary provides names for Richard's challenges by documenting the diagnoses that are applicable to his clinical presentation. These include Specific Learning Disorder with Impairment in Reading based on a lack of word reading accuracy and fluency, also known as dyslexia; Specific Learning Disorder with Impairment in Written Expression based on deficits in spelling accuracy, grammar and clarity of written expression; attention deficit hyperactivity disorder, predominantly inattentive presentation; and generalized anxiety disorder, which appears to be impacting his social interactions. The report also excludes medical or social/environmental factors as contributing factors to the student's challenges. These findings should help guide the appropriate intervention strategies to address his needs.

7 Teach & Treat

Teach

The *teaching and educational intervention* of individuals diagnosed with dyslexia requires three approaches: *Remediation, Accommodations and Modifications.* Remediation emphasizes the strengthening of the student's weaknesses at a fast pace to allow them to narrow or eliminate their academic gap when compared with their classroom peers. This increased rate of skill acquisition is essential to help students "normalize" their reading skills. We shall begin this chapter by describing evidence-based remediation interventions and will follow with descriptions of accommodations and modifications that can help individuals diagnosed with dyslexia. In addition, we will provide some general descriptions of frequently used interventions in addressing some of the most common coexisting conditions.

Remediation

Teaching and remediating students with dyslexia should be based on the science of reading. This approach is designed to address its causes and resulting deficits identified in the definition provided in Chapter 1. That is, in order to address the educational needs of the specific learning disorder that is dyslexia, we must begin by managing the deficits in the phonological components of language. These deficits lead to challenges with the accurate and/or fluent word recognition and spelling. As a result of these difficulties, the student's reading comprehension and reading experience are significantly reduced resulting in limited growth of vocabulary and background knowledge.[1] Given these facts, the focus of how to teach a student diagnosed with dyslexia and related disorders, should emphasize improving literacy skills, including decoding, spelling, fluency and comprehension. This type of reading instruction, based on the science of reading, is also known as **Structured Literacy**. The term *Structured Literacy* was coined by the International Dyslexia Association (IDA) to describe an evidence-based approach to reading instruction. An important concept to understand is that students diagnosed with dyslexia do not need a different teaching approach. Every student will benefit from structured literacy. Those with dyslexia will require a higher intensity of instruction in order to develop the necessary skills to meet curriculum expectations. They will also likely require more time to bring these skills to proficient levels.

The Science of Reading – Structured Literacy

Decades of scientific research provide us with guidance on the most effective ways to teach reading and remediate individuals who struggle with these skills, including those diagnosed with dyslexia (National Reading Panel, 2000[2]; Kilpatrick, 2015; Mather & Wendling, 2012). This body of scientific research indicates that teaching of reading must include *content* (what is taught) and *instructional practices* (how it is taught) that address the specific skills that impact the development of literacy. The content focuses on the five components of literacy, which are these: Phonemic awareness, phonics (letter-sound associations), fluency, vocabulary and comprehension. Thus, this approach will require instruction that includes phonology (the speech sound system), orthography (the writing system/letter-sound relationships), syntax (the structure of sentences), morphology (the meaningful parts of words), semantics (meaning and relationships among words) and discourse (the organization of spoken and written language). These are the foundational elements of Structured Literacy. This is an explicit reading instruction practice that must be delivered in a systematic, cumulative and explicit manner based on the teacher's assessment of the student. That is, the teacher explains and demonstrates key skills in an organized sequence of instruction. We will discuss this approach to intervention based on its three components: Content, instructional practice and assessment (diagnostic teaching).

Content/What to Teach – The Basic Elements of Structured Literacy

Based on the Simple View of Reading (Gough & Tunmer, 1986) and the definition of dyslexia Structured Literacy instruction requires that students are provided with the following skills:

- *Phonology:* This critical element of Structured Literacy instruction provides for the study of the sound structure of the language. It requires the development of phonological awareness skills such as rhyming, counting words in a sentence, clapping syllables and phonemic awareness. The latter refers to the ability of the student to breakdown words into their sounds.
- *Sound-Symbol Association:* After students develop appropriate phonemic awareness of spoken language, they should learn how these sounds relate to the printed words or symbols. This approach is also known as *"phonics"*. This is a "two-way street" learning approach where students learn how to map the sounds (phonemes) to letters or words. The first approach is reading, which goes from the visual to auditory route. The other is spelling which goes from the auditory to the visual route. The acquisition of sound-symbol association skills requires teaching students how to combine or blend sounds and letters into words in order to decode

them. In addition, it allows students to learn how to breakdown or segment words into individual sounds. The instruction of sound-symbol association is provided within language enriched experiences.
- *Syllable Instruction:* The English language has six different types of syllables. These are units of written or oral language with one vowel representing different vowel grapheme types. A grapheme is a symbol, such as a letter or sequence of letters, that represents a sound or phoneme. For example, the sound /t/ is the phoneme represented by the letter 't'. However you may also have letter combinations, like 'igh' that also represent one sound /ī/. This knowledge increases reading accuracy by enhancing the student's awareness of how to decode unfamiliar words. The six types of syllables in the English language are closed, vowel-consonant-e, open, consonant-le, r-controlled and vowel pair.
- *Morphology:* Morphemes are the smallest meaningful unit in a language. These include prefixes, suffixes, infixes, roots and base words. Developing sound morphological skills allows students to decode and understand the meaning of certain words.
- *Syntax:* This represents the rules that determine the sequence and function of the words in a sentence to convey meaning. Syntax requires acquiring knowledge of grammar, sentence structure and the mechanics of language.
- *Semantics:* This is the aspect of language that deals with the meaning of a word, phrase, sentence or text. This requires that, from the start, comprehension needs to be an integral component of reading instruction. After all, we read to understand what the author wrote!

The International Dyslexia Association developed the Knowledge and Practice Standards for Teachers of Reading (KPS) as a guide for teachers. This document details the knowledge that teachers should have in order to teach ALL students how to read effectively. In Chapter 8 we provide resources that describe how to address students with literacy related challenges, including the KPS.

Instructional Practices – When and How to Teach

Reading remediation interventions are most effective if implemented in the first three to four years of their school experience (preschool through second grade) when basic academic skills are the focus of instruction. Findings of a multi-centre study published in Educational Psychology in 2017 (Lovett et al., 2017) indicated that evidence based early intervention in basic reading skills of at-risk students resulted in greater "normalization" of reading scores. The study found that this was particularly true when foundational word reading skills were taught in the first and second grades. These students made twice the gain in reading skills as those whose intervention began in the third grade. Other findings demonstrated that when students were provided the intervention in the first grade, they continued to gain reading skills at a faster rate in subsequent years than those who began intervention in the second and third grades.

Research studies on implementation conducted in some of the lowest performing US schools have demonstrated the efficacy of these types of interventions.[3] All of these remediation approaches to teaching require that the teachers have knowledge of the science of reading and the most effective methods of instruction such as Structured Literacy. Given these findings, providing effective instructional approaches in design (how we teach) and content (what we teach) is critical for the student's success. Some of these instructional practices are described below.

Create a Strategic Classroom Environment: A strategic classroom is one that promotes strategy and skill development. It requires planning, structure and organization. Some of these strategies are describe below.

Demystification: Describing the student's learning style by providing them with a clear explanation and proper terminology to label their symptoms will help them understand their learning profile (strengths and weaknesses). The goal of this approach is to prevent and/or disprove any misconceptions the student may have regarding their learning. A way to accomplish this is by answering the five questions described in the Formulation chapter. This can help demystify the student's misconceptions and provide a better understanding of their strengths and weaknesses. For example, if you were to demystify the learning challenges of Richard, the student described in the case study in the previous chapter, you can begin by acknowledging his strong verbal reasoning skills and provide concrete examples of how he demonstrates this during oral discussions in class. It is also important to explain that he also has some problems. By recognizing that significant difficulties with reading and spelling were identified the demystification process validates Richard's experiences. Helping him understand that these challenges result from his brain's difficulty processing the sounds in the words and this is the most common type of learning problem is critical. Richard should know that his difficulties sounding words has a name, phonemic awareness, and that this is the cause of his reading problem, which is called dyslexia. So, you described the problem, the cause, and gave it a name. You let him know that he is smart but you also acknowledge that there is a reading problem. You can then explain that there is a way to teach him that will help address these difficulties.

Continuing to apply these principles to the case study in the previous chapter, it is also very important to help the student understand that they are not lazy. The challenges they experience with work completion are likely the result of their reading and/or attention difficulties. Because Richard tends to be easily distracted and can "zone out" during work or may struggle to read words, he may find it much harder to complete tasks on time. It is also important to acknowledge that his anxiety can have a significant effect on Richard's academic performance. Identifying anxiety as a factor in his learning may explain the fear and excessive worry that can cause him to feel tense, angry or "freeze" when confronted with stressful situations, like tests or reading out loud. It is equally important to let him know that, while you will make accommodations to help him succeed, you will not change your expectations. That is, Richard's ultimate work product should meet the goals and standards of the classroom. Such an approach empowers the student to assume control of their own learning, increases motivation and teaches them how to learn.

Provide a structured environment: Make sure that students are aware of what is expected of them and why. Describe why you are using a particular strategy to teach a specific skill. Let them know how a new skill is going to be used. Organize the lesson plans by setting goals for the learning, practice and application of these new skills for the day, the week, the month and the school year. Allow extra time to teach the skills and provide relentless supervised practice. Practice will ensure that students will develop the necessary skills to an automatic level in order to perform effectively in school. This type of practice allows you to provide specific feedback in response to a student's mistake or challenge. Finally, grade the students for implementing and practicing these skills and strategies. For example, when studying for a test, award bonus points if the student provides documentation that they implemented the study and test taking strategies that were taught in class. If the student is reading aloud, reward the use of a strategy for decoding an unfamiliar word that you have recently taught.

Provide Explicit and Systematic Instruction: This style of instruction requires a methodical, unambiguous approach to teaching based on effective educational research. Therefore, it is necessary that you explain and demonstrate key skills in a clear manner rather than having the student infer or "discover" these essential skills. It incorporates an appropriate design and engaging delivery of lessons in a direct and clear manner. Explicit instruction requires that the lessons emphasize content that includes essential skills, strategies, vocabulary terms, concepts and rules. This content should be delivered in a systematic logical sequence with easier skills taught before more difficult ones. Start with the skills that are used frequently before introducing those used less often or exceptions to the rules. This approach provides for the teaching of basic/prerequisite skills first, until they are developed to an automatic level. Finally, explicit instruction benefits from breaking down or "chunking" the more complex skills and strategies into easier instructional units.

Students who experience the greatest reading challenges will need additional small group instruction time to "catch up". This is necessary to ensure that they have a solid foundation on letter and sound knowledge as well as overall language skills.

Assessment – Diagnostic Teaching

Structured Literacy requires the teacher to evaluate students at regular intervals in order to identify the skills and functions that need remediation and to monitor the student's academic progress and response to intervention strategies. Ascertaining the student's level of literacy skills is therefore essential to providing them with appropriate teaching interventions. As noted in Chapter 4, many schools administer yearly universal assessments in the fall, winter and spring to determine the student's needs and to ascertain if they are meeting specific benchmarks or curriculum goals throughout the school year. This is an essential component of the RTI model. The RTI model requires that all students are provided with evidence-based reading instruction in a typical classroom setting (Tier-1). Students identified as reading below grade level (regardless of the cause) are enrolled in supplementary small group instruction on Tier-2 or Tier-3 for a period of 20–30 minutes per day, one of more days per week, based on their level of difficulty with reading. Using screening instruments like the DIBELS, EarlyBird and other standardized instruments, the teachers identify the weakest reading skill of each student in order to determine the starting point of their intervention. In the case of older students and adults, teachers may choose to use a method such as the University of Florida Lastinger Centre for Learning Diagnostic Model that was described in Chapter 4. Using this approach, the teacher identifies the student's lowest skill mastered and begins to provide small group intervention at that level.

In summary, Structured Literacy is a method of instruction that is based on the science of reading that is effective for all students. In the case of those diagnosed with dyslexia, the teachers must provide more time and intensity to help students develop and improve literacy skills. The International Dyslexia Association developed the Knowledge and Practice Standards for Teachers of Reading which is a wonderful resource for those interested in providing evidence-based instruction.

Accommodations

Accommodations use the student's strengths and interests to help them overcome their difficulties. While remediation focuses on strengthening the student's weaknesses in specific skills in an accelerated fashion to narrow the performance gap in achievement between the student and their peers, accommodations emphasize promoting and developing the student's strengths while accommodating their learning needs in order to accomplish a goal. Accommodations are usually provided in three forms: Extended time, assistive technology and individual assistance. We will provide a brief description of them below.

- *Extended time:* This is a frequently used accommodation particularly effective when a student must read complex text in a defined time frame. It is often provided during classroom tests and other types of tests, such as college admissions, licensing and certification examinations. Given the difficulties with decoding and fluency in students with dyslexia, this is an accommodation that does not change the complexity of the task but allows the student to read at their own pace. It also allows the student to use and practice their language comprehension skills, a strength for those diagnosed with dyslexia. Thus, the expectation has not changed (get a high enough score to pass), but the student was allowed the accommodation of extended time. This is a type of accommodation that is also frequently used by students who experience difficulty with efficient work production, such as those diagnosed with ADHD and/or anxiety.

- *Assistive Technology and Alternative Formats:* The advent of computers has brought a series of tools that were not available several years ago. For example, text-to-voice technology allows students to "read" a text or a test question. Many of the textbooks now exist in electronic form that allows the use of this technology. Similarly, tests administered in an electronic format may allow for this type of accommodation. Assistive technology allows these students to meet the same expectations as other students by facilitating "reading" the same number of books and answering the same questions as other students. The only difference is that an accommodation was provided to allow for their neurodevelopmental difficulties. The opposite technology, voice-to-text, provides for the student to "write" without having to be concerned about spelling or handwriting challenges. This is a common technology that it is used by many professionals without reading disabilities. For example, electronic medical records allow the doctors to dictate their reports, eliminating the need for a transcriptionist. This is also a very useful technology in distance learning and online meetings where the use of closed captioning is often provided to ensure that the content is understood by all. Assistive technology is a common element of universal design that is useful to all, but essential for those with specific challenges, thus allowing unrestricted access to written content for all. However, it is very important to be judicious in the application of assistive technology to ensure that if a skill is required to perform a particular function essential for that course or job, the person is able to fulfil those requirements. For example, a person who cannot do mental math quickly may not be able to calculate accurate doses of medications in an emergency where assistive technology may not be available. In those circumstances, the accommodation of using a calculator on a licensing exam may not be allowed as it would change the expectation of the job. This is also the case on accommodating for the volume of work as it may impact graduation requirements, especially in higher education.

Allowing the student to complete work on content subjects that gives them the opportunity to use their strengths is another way to accommodate to their specific learning needs. For example, a student diagnosed with dyslexia may have significant difficulty writing a book report or an essay on a history assignment. However, they are particularly skilled in the use of PowerPoint and have strong oral language skills. In such a situation, where the goal is assessing the student's content knowledge, an oral presentation that includes PowerPoint slides may be an alternative way to

demonstrate mastery of the content. There are many other different ways in which teachers can allow students to document knowledge using an alternative format.
- *Personal Assistance:* This is a frequently used accommodation in schools and work, especially when assistive technology is not available or difficult to use. A common example is the use of a scribe for note taking or having a reader read the questions on a test. If the individual can't read but has a good understanding of the subject matter, they may be able to answer questions on the test. This would allow the teacher to evaluate the student's content knowledge even though the student can't read.

Modifications

Another way to assist students diagnosed with dyslexia is to provide them with simple **modifications.** These are typically offered to students from preschool through the high/secondary school. They usually consist of grading only for content and not taking points off for spelling, avoiding embarrassing situations, decreasing the volume of work and other strategies. Some of these modifications are summarized below.

- *Avoid embarrassment* by asking the students to read out loud or write in front of the class. If they can demonstrate significant content knowledge in oral work, they will gain confidence from being asked to provide verbal answers during the course of the lesson.
- *Collaborating with a dyslexia specialist* can help the classroom teacher implement programmes specifically designed by the specialist in place of unsuitable literacy work for the student's level of reading and writing competence. This helps the class teacher and reduces the shame and embarrassment of the child who is unable to achieve in these areas at an appropriate level.
- Even the most zealous teacher would want to *avoid a profusion of spelling corrections* in bright red ink that can be demoralizing to a student diagnosed with dyslexia. Spelling corrections are necessary and can be useful, but a yellow highlighter can be more desirable than red ink and can isolate the part of the word that is misspelt. Similarly, if the goal of the task is to assess the student's knowledge of a content subject, the work can be graded without taking points away for spelling mistakes. Overall, students will likely show greater progress in spelling when provided with their own individual learning programme based on the science of reading.
- *Establishing a homework policy* that is mutually agreed between home and school can be very useful. Homework assignments can take a long time to complete. When other family members become involved, dread of these demands can cast a long shadow. There is much more at stake than the completion of any particular assignment. Homework is not supposed to be a curse, yet it can colour students' attitudes towards school and adversely affect their motivation for the years ahead if it is allowed to become one. Modified homework requirements therefore can have a long-term positive

effect by bringing balance to the student's work/home life. Limitations as to time spent or quantity done are useful, as is the provision of alternative work. A child can be given the same requirements but with the instruction that not more than an agreed upon amount of time each night should be spent on them. This will necessitate allowing for unfinished work, fewer number of math problems, spelling words, books to read or reports to write. These types of modifications can have an impact on graduation requirements particularly at the university level. Another option for homework completion is to break an assignment into smaller "chunks" and allow the student to complete it in stages. As their skill level in reading and spelling improves, the amount of homework can also be increased.

Treat

In addition to providing evidence-based instruction, teachers are often required to address some of the student's coexisting condition(s) identified in the assessment. These other factors are part of the Treatment of a student diagnosed with dyslexia. Addressing all the areas of impairment, educational, behavioural emotional, social interaction and health is essential when we consider the "whole child" perspective.

As we mentioned earlier in this book, dyslexia is often accompanied by many coexisting conditions. In the previous chapter, Formulation, we explained the critical importance of identifying other factors that can impact learning and its management. For the purpose of this chapter, we will briefly address the Treatment of problems of attention, behaviour and emotional regulation, and health based on the Rule of Fours.

Attention Problems (ADHD)

- *Educational Management:* Many of the most common strategies to assist students with ADHD are provided as accommodations. Some of the most common ones include preferential seating, extended time on testing, the use of assistive technology and organizational support. Preferential seating is helpful to ensure the student's attention, facilitate compliance and management of disruptive behaviours. Given that students with ADHD experience problems with efficient production and completion of work due to distractibility and impulsivity, extended time on testing and/or allowing them to take a test in a quiet environment can be of great help to them. To assist with personal organization, a life skills coach can be helpful. This is an individual who would provide the student with ideas on how to organize and maintain their work productivity. The use of calendars, cell phone applications and timers can be useful in this regard.
- *Psychological Management:* Behaviour modification is the most common non-medical intervention provided to children diagnosed with ADHD.

This approach requires that the adults change the way that they interact with the child for the child to change their response to the adults. The goal of behaviour modification is to improve compliance. Compliance is defined as doing what you were told to do when you were told to do it, typically a few seconds after a command. We have provided some references in the resource chapter on this topic.

- *Medical Management:* Stimulant medications are the most common medicines used in the management of ADHD. The American Academy of Pediatrics[4] recommends prescribing medications in conjunction with or following behaviour modification. For more information on these medications, please refer to the resource section of this book. Ensuring appropriate sleep for a child with attention difficulties is also quite important. For if a child does not have sufficient sleep, they will likely not be sufficiently alert to pay attention in school.
- *Environmental Management:* As noted above, preferential seating and taking tests in an environment with minimal distractions can be very helpful. In addition, having an organized classroom, where everything is in its place and providing a visual schedule can make it easier for these students to work. Similarly, the parents can also provide a structured schedule at home to ensure that there is a specific time to complete homework and to organize the child's school bag, go to sleep and eat meals at appropriate times.

Behavioural/Emotional Challenges

- Psychological therapy is the hallmark of behaviour and emotional management. As we previously described, there are three types of behaviour disorders: Internalizers, externalizers and atypical disorders.

    - *Internalizing disorders*
        - *Educational interventions:* Students with anxiety and depression may benefit from reassurance provided in the form of allowing them to ask questions in private and to "give them permission" to fail and try again. However, if the anxiety and low self-esteem are the result of a learning disorder, providing them with evidence-based instruction is the best treatment of choice.
        - *Psychological Therapy:* Cognitive behaviour therapy is the most common approach to addressing these types of disorders. In this type of psychological therapy, the goal is to help individuals change the way that they think about how they feel. In other words, this method emphasizes a change in perspective to focus on what the person can do to address a specific problem. Teaching the child how to recognize and identify their symptoms and the strategies that can help manage them is very effective. This type of therapy is usually short-term in duration and requires

that the parents and teachers learn how to coach the students to implement the strategies that help them manage their symptoms. Cognitive behaviour therapy is similar to the way Structured Literacy is implemented in the approach to instruction. It is performed in a structured and systematic fashion (the "how to") and addresses the specific anxiety symptoms (the "what") of the child.

- *Medical Management:* The most common medications that are used in the management of these disorders are often referred to as antidepressants due to their first use, but many of them are also quite effective in managing anxiety. They are also known by the acronym SSRI (Selective Serotonin Reuptake Inhibitors) which describe the neurotransmitter (serotonin) that they impact. Please refer to the resource section of this book for more information on these medications. Typically, medication management is used in the treatment of disorders such as ADHD, anxiety, depression and agitation. They are often provided in conjunction with psychological therapy. Most psychiatric medications treat the symptoms and do not "cure" any of the disorders.

- *Externalizing disorders:* In the section above we described behaviour modification as a strategy that is effective for adults to manage children with ADHD. This is also the treatment of choice in the management of externalizing behaviours, such as oppositionality, defiance, lying, stealing and other antisocial behaviours. We have provided references in the resource section of this book to help address these problems.

- *Medical problems:* Other conditions that may warrant medical intervention include sleep difficulties, encopresis (soiling of the underwear) and enuresis (night and daytime wetting) and changing medications that may be affecting the student's performance in school (making them too sleepy or irritable). Bringing these symptoms to the doctor's attention is very important and quite helpful in the management of the student's medical conditions.

Notes

1 https://dyslexiaida.org/definition-of-dyslexia
2 www.nichd.nih.gov/publications/pubs/nrp/smallbook
3 Perspectives of Language and Literacy Summer 2021.
4 www.AAP.org

8 Useful Resources

We classified the resources in this chapter according to the order of the chapters of the book itself for ease of reference.

Chapter 1 Resources

- The International Dyslexia Association: https://dyslexiaida.org
- The British Dyslexia Association: www.bdadyslexia.org.uk
- The National Reading Panel: www.nichd.nih.gov
- Learning Disability Association of America (LDA): www.LDAlearning.com
- American Academy of Paediatrics: www.healthychildren.org/English/health-issues/conditions/learning-disabilities
- Canada Dyslexia Association: www.dyslexiaassociation.ca
- Understood: www.understood.org/
- Reading Rockets: www.readingrockets.org/
- Mindroom: www.mindroom.org
- Teaching Reading Through Spelling (Kingston Programme): http://www.ldalearning.com
- Handwriting without Tears: A programme for teaching the movement skills of letter-formation in the early years and strengthening the fine motor skills involved: www.hwtears.com

Chapter 3 Resources

Early Developmental and Academic Questionnaire

- *Infancy*
    - Say single words by 12 months (e.g., drink, juice, mommy)
    - Understand 250 words by 18 months
    - Speak in two-to-three-word phrases by two years (e.g., go car, want cookie)

- *After completing four-year-old prekindergarten*
    - Identify words that rhyme with each other (e.g., run/fun) and enjoying rhyming games

DOI: 10.4324/9781003212058-8

- Name most uppercase letters
- Identify the letters in their name

- *After completing Kindergarten*
  - Name all of the lowercase letters
  - Say the sound of most letters
  - Match a beginning sound to a word starting with that sound (e.g., /sss/ to sun)
  - Identify the beginning sounds of spoken words
  - Read a simple C-V-C word (e.g., pat)
  - Write their first and last name
  - Spell simple C-V-C words
  - Have age/grade appropriate vocabulary knowledge (knows as many words as their peers)

- *After completing the first grade*
  - Separate and/or count the sounds in a word
  - Sound out unfamiliar words while reading
  - Spell assigned words correctly
  - Understand stories and instructions as well as their classmates
  - Clearly communicate thoughts and ideas orally
  - Understand what others mean by what they say

- *After completing the second grade*
  - Read rapidly, accurately and with good intonation
  - Spell most grade level words appropriately, individually and when writing in sentences

Typical School Day Questionnaire

- *Morning Routine*
  - Waking up
    - Significant difficulty waking up in the morning
  - Getting dressed
    - Difficulty getting dressed because of distractions (e.g., told to get dressed and a few minutes later the child is still in pyjamas playing with a toy or with a pet and forgot to get dressed – not defiant, just forgetful)
    - Difficulty buttoning, snapping, tying or zipping
  - Breakfast
    - Difficulty sitting still through breakfast
    - Difficulty handling silverware

- Disruptive during breakfast
- Very messy while eating
- Leaving for School
  - Difficulty/Forgetful gathering materials (book bag, lunch, sports uniform, homework)
  - Rarely on time
- Arriving at school
  - Forgets materials in car/bus
  - Does not remember classroom morning routine
  - Significant difficulty separating from parents (scared, crying, panicked)

- *Evening Routine*
  - Arriving at home
    - Follows routine appropriately (changing clothes, snack, etc.)
    - Extreme behaviour responses (irritable, tantrums, etc.)
  - Homework
    - Has necessary homework materials
    - Completes homework independently
    - Remembers to pack homework in book bag
    - Remembers to turn in homework the next day
  - Extracurricular activities
    - Any difficulty or problems during sports, music lessons, etc.
  - Supper Time
    - Difficulty sitting or sitting still through the meal
    - Handling silverware
  - Bedtime
    - Trouble falling asleep
    - Trouble staying asleep
    - Frequent nightmares

Peer Interactions Questionnaire

- Any difficulty
  - Making friends
  - Keeping friends
- Shows poor sportsmanship
- Aggressive towards other children

- Bossy
- Withdrawn/Extremely shy
- Prefers children who are:
  - Younger
  - Older
  - Same age

Health and Family History Questionnaire: These should be mostly YES/NO responses as the teacher does not need to know the details, only if there are any concerns.

- Early history
  - Any significant *complications* before, during or after birth?
- Medical History
  - Any significant illnesses that can affect school attendance or student's stamina
  - Any medications that can impact alertness, mood or health
  - Any allergies that the school should be aware of (this needs to be a specific response, i.e., what is the student allergic to?)
- Family History
  - Any family history in close relatives (parents, siblings, grandparents, aunts/uncles or cousins) with learning problems or related disorders? Specify that you do not want to know who, just if there is a history.
  - Does this child remind you of anyone in the family?

Social History Questionnaire: These should be mostly YES/NO responses as the teacher does not need to know the details, only if there are any concerns.

- Has the family experienced any of these situations during the last year?
  - Birth of a child
  - Death of a relative
  - Serious health problems in a close relative
  - Marital difficulties, separation or divorce
  - Change of a job
  - Move/relocation
  - Financial difficulties

Chapter 4 Resources

Screening Tools

- *The Dyslexia Screener*, by Martin Turner and Pauline Smith (2004), computerizes the methodology by means of which teachers who train with

70 Useful Resources

Dyslexia Action learn to assess children on the Certificate and Diploma courses. For more information, see: www.nfer-nelson.co.uk
- The National Center for Improving Literacy: Excellent source of evidence-based approaches to screen, identify and teach students with literacy-related disabilities, including dyslexia: https://improvingliteracy.org
- RTI Network: Universal Screening for Reading Problems & Progress Monitoring: www.rtinetwork.org
- National Center on Intensive Intervention: https://intensiveintervention.org/
- Reading Fluency Assessment: Error Analysis through Passage Fluency Reading (IRIS Center, Vanderbilt University): https://iris.peabody.vanderbilt.edu/module/dbi2/cresource/q2/p06/
- Fluency Norms: by grade/time of year: https://www.readingrockets.org/article/fluency-norms-chart-2017-update

Chapter 5 Resources

Standardized Assessment Instruments: Different tests for dyslexia look at different skills related to reading which include skills such as decoding, reading fluency and reading comprehension. Here are some examples of the tests associated with them which can be used by teachers:

1. *Letter-sound knowledge*[1]: Letter-sound knowledge refers to the student's familiarity with letter forms, names and corresponding sounds, which may be measured by recognition, production and writing tasks. To assess letter-name fluency, students may be given a list made up of random uppercase and lowercase letters and then requested to identify the names of as many letters as they possibly can in just one minute. Another similar test is of letter-sound fluency, where students are given a list of random uppercase and lowercase letters and allowed only one minute to identify as many letter sounds as they possibly can. Students may also be requested to write letters that are dictated or write the letter or letter combination that corresponds to a sound that is presented orally by their teachers (such as to write the letter that makes the /l/ sound for example). Some of the tests that can measure such an ability include the following:

    - Woodcock-Johnson IV Tests of Achievement (Word Attack, Spelling of Sounds).
    - Kaufman Test of Educational Achievement, 3rd ed. (Letter Naming Facility, Letter Checklist).
    - Process Assessment of the Learner, 2nd ed. (Letters).
    - Wechsler Individual Achievement Test, 3rd ed. (Naming Letters, Letter-Sound Correspondence).

2. *Word Decoding:* It is important to measure students' word-reading skills. Word reading skills can be measured by assessing accuracy and fluency

and both real and nonsense words in timed and untimed situations can be used. Untimed tests of both real and nonsense word reading provide information regarding whether the student has reached the required word-reading accuracy or not and about the letter-sound correspondences of English; i.e., phonics while timed tests provide information regarding whether the student has fluency in their word identification ability or not. Some of the measures that can assess such an ability include the following:

- Test of Word Reading Efficiency-2 (TOWRE-2)
- Woodcock-Johnson IV Tests of Achievement (Letter-Word Identification).
- Kaufman Test of Educational Achievement, 3rd ed. (Letter and Word Naming).
- Wechsler Individual Achievement Test, 3rd ed. (Word Reading).
- Macmillan Graded Word Reading Test (ca 6–14) NFER-Nelson, 1985.
- Wide Range Achievement Test, 3rd ed. (ca 5–75) Jastak Associates, 1993.
- WRAPS Word Recognition and Phonic Skills (ca 4–8) Hodder & Stoughton, 1994.

3. *Reading Fluency:* Reading fluency is simply the speed or the rate at which students read words or passages accurately. Both oral and silent reading fluency can be measured. Tests used to assess fluency tend to measure reading rate more specifically. Reading rate comprises both word-level automaticity and the speed and fluidity with which a reader moves through connected text (Hudson Kam & Newport, 2005). Automaticity is quick and effortless identification of words in or out of context (Ehri & McCormick, 1998; Stahl & Kuhn, 2002). Measuring reading rate should encompass consideration of both single-word reading automaticity and reading speed in connected text. Assessment of automaticity can include tests of sight-word knowledge or tests of decoding rate. Tests of decoding rate often consist of rapid decoding of nonwords. Measurement of nonword reading rate ensures that the construct being assessed is the student's ability to automatically decode words using letter-sound knowledge (Hudson Kam & Newport, 2005) as opposed to rapid recognition of real words that the student has memorized. Measures that can be used to assess these skills include the following:

- Woodcock-Johnson IV Tests of Achievement (Oral Reading, Sentence Reading Fluency).
- Test of Word Reading Efficiency – 2 (Sight Word Efficiency, Phonemic Decoding Efficiency).
- Kaufman Test of Educational Achievement, 3rd ed. (Word Recognition Fluency).
- Decoding Fluency.

- Silent Reading Fluency.
- Process Assessment of the Learner, 2nd ed. (RAN-Words, Morphological Decoding Fluency, Sentence Sense).
- Wechsler Individual Achievement Test, 3rd ed. (Oral Reading Fluency).
- Gray Oral Reading Tests, 5th ed. (Rate, Fluency).
- Nelson Denny Reading Test (Silent Reading): Good instrument for students in high school and college.

4. *Spelling (Encoding):* Spelling tests provide information regarding students' understanding of and ability to apply phonics to the spelling of words and of a student's orthographic and morphological awareness (Berninger, 2007). Spelling tests are used to determine whether a student uses correct or incorrect letter combinations and whether the student's spellings reflect knowledge of conventions. Spelling tests also provide information regarding students' morphological awareness. While tests that ask students to spell nonsense words are less common, they tend to be useful in assessing a student's knowledge of phonics. Measures that are used to assess such an ability include the following:

- Woodcock-Johnson IV Tests of Achievement (Spelling).
- Kaufman Test of Educational Achievement, 3rd ed. (Spelling).
- Process Assessment of the Learner, 2nd ed. (Word Choice).
- Wechsler Individual Achievement Test, 3rd ed. (Spelling).
- British Spelling Test Series 1–5 (ca 5–24) NFER-Nelson, 1996.
- Diagnostic Spelling Test (ca 7–11) Vincent & Claydon, NFER-Nelson, 1982.
- Parallel Spelling Tests (ca 6–15) Young, Hodder & Stoughton, 1983.
- Spelling in Context – Peters & Smith, Windsor: NFER-Nelson 1990.
- Wide Range Achievement Test, 3rd ed. (ca 5–75) Jastak Associates, 1993.

5. *Reading Comprehension:* Reading comprehension tests can be individually administered as part of a comprehensive evaluation or can be group administered and the reading comprehension measures do also vary in the type of text students are expected to read; i.e., narrative, informational or persuasive. It goes without saying that students perform differently depending on the mode of administration, or the type of text or in the format of the test itself. According to the formats, reading comprehension tests can be further classified into cloze, question answering and retelling. Cloze format tests present sentences or passages with blanks in them and the student is expected to read the text and provide an appropriate word to go in the blank. Tests with a question-answer format require students to read passages and answer

questions about them. Retellings simply require students to read a text and then orally tell teachers about what was just read. Some of the tests that can measure such an ability include the following:

- Woodcock-Johnson IV Tests of Achievement (Passage Comprehension, Reading Recall, Reading Vocabulary).
- Kaufman Test of Educational Achievement, 3rd ed. (Reading Comprehension, Oral Language).
- Process Assessment of the Learner, 2nd ed.
- Wechsler Individual Achievement Test, 3rd ed. (Reading Comprehension).
- The Suffolk Reading Scale, 2nd ed. (ca 6–7, ca 8–10 & ca 11–14) NFER-Nelson, 2001.
- Wide Span Reading Test – revised (ca 7–14) Brimer, NFER-Nelson, 1984·
- Macmillan Individual Reading Analysis (ca 5–10) Vincent & de la Mare, NFER-Nelson, 1990.
- Listening and Literacy Index (ca 6–9) Weedon & Reid, Hodder & Stoughton, 2001.
- Nelson-Denny: (Vocabulary and Comprehension): Good instrument for students in high school and college that assesses timed and untimed comprehension.

6. *Phonological Awareness*[2]: Phonological awareness is an extremely important component that needs to be assessed when identifying dyslexia. It refers simply to the student's awareness of as well as their access to the sound structure of their oral language. Phonological awareness is often considered one of the principal difficulties in dyslexia. Research studies have consistently shown that children who are weak in phonological awareness display improved reading performance after being given intervention designed to improve their phonological awareness (Torgesen et al., 1992, 1997). Some of the tests that can measure this ability include the following:

- Comprehensive Test of Phonological Processes (2nd Edition).
- NEPSY-II Phonological Processing subtest.
- Phonological Assessment Battery – Frederickson et al., (ca: 6–15) NFER-Nelson, 1995.
- Phonological Abilities Test (ca 4–7) Muter, Hulme & Snowling, The Psychological Corporation, 1991.
- Preschool and Primary Inventory of Phonological Awareness (ca 3–6 11/12 – Dodd et al.
- Test of Phonological Awareness (ca 5–8) – Torgesen & Bryant, The Psychological Corporation, 1994.
- Pupils' Test of Non-Word Repetition (4–8) Gathercool & Baddely, The Psychological Corporation, 1996.

- Graded Non-Word Reading Test, Snowling et al., Thames Valley Test Company, 1996.
- K-TEA Supplemental Composites (Sound-Symbol, Decoding).

7. *Rapid Automatized Naming Test:*
   - Speeded Naming subtest of NEPSY-II
   - Rapid Picture Naming subtest of WJ III
   - Rapid Colour, Letter and Digit naming subtests of the CTOPP-2

8. *Behaviour Questionnaires:*

   a. **Global Behaviour Scales**
      - ASEBA: The Achenbach System of Empirically Based Assessment is "a comprehensive evidence-based assessment system developed through decades of research and practical experience. The ASEBA assesses competencies, strengths, adaptive functioning; behavioural, emotional and social problems from age 1½ to over 90 years". For school-age children, ASEBA offers a Parent/Caregiver Report Form (CBCL – ages 6 to 18), a Teacher Report Form (TRF – ages 6 to 18) and a Youth Self Report Form (YSR – ages 11 to 18). There are also Preschool forms available. These forms have been translated into 110 languages.
      - BASC-3: The Behaviour Assessment System for Children – Third Edition is a "comprehensive set of rating scales and forms, BASC-3 helps you understand the behaviours and emotions of children and adolescents". Like the ASEBA, the BASC offers Teacher Rating Scales (TRS), Parent Rating Scales (PRS) and Self-Report of Personality (SRP). The BASC is available in English and Spanish.

   b. **Disorder Specific Scales**
      - ADHD
         - Conners 3rd Edition: One of the most used ADHD assessment instruments. Available in short and long versions for parents, teachers and students. It has been translated into multiple languages: www.pearsonassessments.com
         - Vanderbilt ADHD Diagnostic Rating Scale has parent and teacher rating scales and can be downloaded for free from the NICHQ (National Institute for Children Health Quality). It is an easy to score questionnaire: https://www.nichq.org/sites/default/files/resource-file/NICHQ-Vanderbilt-Assessment-Scales.pdf
         - Brown Attention Deficit Disorder Scales: These scales offer a consistent measure of ADD across the life span based on

Thomas Brown's model of cognitive impairment in ADD, including executive functioning: www.pearsonassessments.com/store/usassessments

- Anxiety & Depression:
    - Screen for Child Anxiety Related Disorders (SCARED – 41 items) provides a teen and parent version that addresses symptoms of Panic Disorder/Somatization, Generalized Anxiety Disorder, Separation Anxiety Disorder, Social Anxiety Disorder, and Significant School Avoidance. It can be obtained free of charge with permission: birmaherb@msx.upmc.edu
    - Generalized Anxiety Disorder 7 item (GAD-7): www.hiv.uw.edu/page/mental-health-screening/gad-7
    - Mental health for children, teenagers and young adults: www.nhs.uk/mental-health/children-and-young-adults
    - Anxiety and Depression in Children: www.cdc.gov/childrensmentalhealth/depression.html
    - Anxiety Disorders: https://kidshealth.org/en/parents/anxiety-disorders.html
    - Columbia Depression Scale (Parent and Teen forms – 22 questions) from the DISC (Diagnostic Interview Schedule for Children) can be obtained free with permission: fisherp@nyspi.columbia.edu
    - Kutcher Adolescent Depression Scale (Teen form – six questions) can be obtained free with permission: https://mentalhealthliteracy.org/wp-content/uploads/2014/09/6-KADS.pdf

Chapter 7 Resources

- The Centre for Effective Reading Instruction: An IDA subsidiary that provides certification to teachers and reading interventionists that affirms their knowledge and skills in teaching literacy using a structured approach to language: www.effectivereading.org
- The Orton-Gillingham Academy: www.ortonacademy.org
- The Reading League: www.thereadingleague.org
- ASHA: American Speech-Language-Hearing Association: www.asha.org
- Dyslexia Action: www.dyslexiaaction.org.uk
- Council for the Registration of Schools Teaching Dyslexic Pupils: www.crested.org.uk
- Creative Learning Company New Zealand: www.creativelearningcentre.com
- Family Onwards: www.familyonwards.com

- Learning Disability Worldwide: www.LDWorldwide.org
- Dyslexia Association of Ireland: www.dyslexia.ie
- Fun Track Learning Centre: www.funtrack.com.au
- Crossbow Education: www.crossboweducation.com
- Literacy development at home and school: https://improvingliteracy.org/brief
- Nemours Reading BrightStart!: Child Care and Preschool Curriculum https://classroom.kidshealth.org/classroom
- EarlyBird: Screening and intervention for dyslexia from K through 1st grade: https://earlybirdeducation.com
- Independent Teacher Training Programs Accredited by IDA https://dyslexiaida.org/accredited-teaching-training-programs/
- University Programs Accredited by IDA https://dyslexiaida.org/university-programs-accredited-by-ida
- Learning Disability Association of America: https://ldaamerica.org/
- IMSLEC: The International Multisensory Structured Language Education Council is a non-profit entity whose goal is to "accredit quality training courses for the professional preparation of multisensory structured language education specialists". IMSLEC provides a directory of accredited programmes on their website. www.imslec.org/directory.asp
- *Units of Sound:* Walter Bramley's *Units of Sound*[3] is a structured, cumulative audio-visual reading, spelling and comprehension programme, for ages 9 and above.
- Jolly Phonics: Developed from **Sue Lloyd**'s *Phonics Handbook*, a series of seven books, *Finger Phonics*, and a wall frieze from Jolly Learning are highly suitable alternative for the initial teaching of reading in a multisensory way.
- *Toe by Toe:* A phonics-based system of reading tuition which seeks to establish a basis of good decoding skills. *Toe By Toe* is published by the author, Keda Cowling: www.kedapublications.co.uk
- Wilson Reading System: The Wilson Reading System® (WRS) is the flagship programme of Wilson Language Training® and the foundation of all other Wilson programmes. WRS is an intensive Tier 3 programme for students in grades 2–12 and adults with word-level deficits who are not making sufficient progress through their current intervention: www.wilsonlanguage.com
- *Dancing Bears:* A newer product than *Toe-by-Toe*,[4] *Dancing Bears* is a complete alphabetic programme for beginners (Level A) that rises to Key Stage 2 and beyond.
- The Sonday System: The Sonday System incorporates the characteristics of Structured Literacy. Winsor Learning provides Orton-Gillingham Sonday System Programs and Training at: https://members.winsorlearning.com
- THRASS: THRASS, or the Teaching of Handwriting, Reading and Spelling Skills, is an integrated system for teaching literacy skills in an alphabetic, systematic way.
- Lifeboat: A well-worked out multisensory phonic scheme for reading and spelling is *The Lifeboat Scheme* ("launch the lifeboat to read and spell") by

Sula and Tony Ellis, and Jackie and Mick Davison, published by: www.robinswood.co.uk
- ALK: The Active Literacy Kit (ALK) is a programme that can be obtained from: www.ldalearning.com
- Barton Reading: An Orton Gillingham Reading Programme: https://bartonreading.com
- S.P.I.R.E: Another well-known Orton-Gillingham fellow's programme: https://eps.schoolspecialty.com/spire
- LiPS from Lindamood-Bell: LiPS is usually taught at Lindamood-Bell centres, but can be used at home too: https://lindamoodbell.com/
- LETRS® Professional Learning for Educators: https://www.lexialearning.com

Vocabulary and Grammar

A variety of resources exists in the US to build vocabulary and sentence structure in younger and older children:

- *100% Concepts – Primary* (ages 5 to 9) and *Intermediate* (suitable for ages 10–14) – contains work that teaches higher-level concepts, including location and direction, quality or condition, comparison, time and occurrence and relationship.
- *100% Story Writing* (ages 8 to 11) gives pupils strategies to sequence, plan and write stories. Work on organizing thoughts before writing, sequencing story events, writing paragraphs and using storyboards to visualize a story.
- *Grammar Shuffle* (ages 9 to 14) consists of games played with five full card decks, one for each of these areas: Noun/Verb Agreement, Sentence Completion, Adjectives, Adverbs, and Compound and Complex Sentences. Grammar Shuffle Junior enables similar activities for the 6 to 10 age range.
- *125 Vocabulary Builders* (ages 10 to 15) teaches pupils how to recognize, learn and integrate new words into their daily vocabulary. Pupils are given strategies for connecting new vocabulary words to each other, to the curriculum and to their prior experience.
- *The Idiom Game* (ages 10 to 16) enables pupils to practice with 800 of the most commonly used idiomatic expressions in our language. Each card provides a multiple-choice question at a lower and upper level. Questions review and build upon learning idioms in four question categories: Definition, same meaning, origin and challenge questions.
- *Grammar Scramble* (ages from 8 to adult) is a scrabble-type board game that operates in crossword fashion. Pupils build intersecting sentences in crossword style. They receive word tiles divided into these parts of speech: Nouns, verbs, pronouns, adjectives, adverbs, articles, interrogatives, prepositions and conjunctions. Each tile has a value: The higher the value, the harder it is to use in a sentence.

Useful Resources

- *Help for Vocabulary* (ages from 8 to adult) teaches these vocabulary areas: Identifying nouns, verbs, adjectives, and adverbs; forming compound words; choosing correct definitions; matching words and definitions; defining with context clues; completing sentences with appropriate words and substituting synonyms in paragraphs. Pupils expand their word knowledge and learn to apply vocabulary skills in context.

Reading Fluency Intervention

- 7 Must-Have Resources to Improve Reading Fluency Right Now: https://www.scholastic.com/teachers/teaching-tools/articles/7-must-have-resources-to-improve-reading-fluency-right-now.html
- *Four Steps to Building Fluency with Text* – National Centre for Improving Literacy: https://improvingliteracy.org/brief/four-steps-building-fluency-text
- *Developing Fluent Readers* – Reading Rockets: https://www.readingrockets.org/article/developing-fluent-readers

Assistive Technology Applications

- Claro Read Assistive technology for reading, writing, note taking and math: www.clarosoftware.com
- Read & Write & Text Help: Assistive technology resources for all educational levels – primary to higher education – and the workplace: www.texthelp.com
- Text Assist: Mind mapping technology to assist with written expression: www.mindmaker.com
- Wynn 2: Assistive technology for reading/visually impaired individuals of all ages: www.freedomscientific.com
- Dolphin Easy Tutor: Accessibility products for use at home and school for visually and reading impaired individuals of all ages: www.yourdolphin.com
- Inspiration: Mind mapping technology to assist with written expression: www.dyslexic.com
- Word Shark: Game based software to assist with reading and spelling: www.wordshark.co.uk
- Rapid Reading: Assistant Design for students who have completed Fast-ForWord Reading series. It helps students in development of fluency, vocabulary and comprehension: www.gemmlearning.com/programs
- Lucid Products: Website provides multiple assessments of reading and other educationally relevant areas: www.lucid-research.com
- Earobics: Interactive software that provides students in prekindergarten through grade three with individual, systematic instruction in early literacy skills
- Lexia Peer reviewed: Structured Literacy interactive software application used in combination with teacher-led instruction: www.lexialearning.com
- Kurzweil: Text-to-speech software with scanning capabilities, communication and productivity. It provides online books and magazines and notetaking, outlining and summarizing programmes: www.kurzweiledu.com

Useful Resources

- Ukandu Series: Assistive technology that includes reading and writing support, evaluation and curriculum: www.donjohnston.com
- Living Books: Educational software products from primary to secondary school. Includes Mavis Beacon Typing programme: www.broderbund.com
- Audible: Very popular audiobooks software: www.audible.com
- IANSYT Ltd.: Website provides software, computers, devices and peripherals to students with disabilities. Some of these products are covered through the Disabled Student's Allowance, a UK government grant for students with disabilities enrolled in higher education: www.iansyst.co.uk & www.dyslexic.com

Dyspraxia

- Dyspraxia Foundation: www.dyspraxiafoundation.org.uk
- Dyspraxia Support Group: www.dyspraxia.org.nz

AD(H)D

- Attention Deficit Disorder Association: www.chadd.org & www.add.org
- The National Attention Deficit Disorder Information and Support Service (ADDISS): www.addiss.co.uk
- ADHD books: www.adders.org and www.addwarehouse.com
- Organization: www.additudemag.com

Medications for Behaviour/Emotional Disorders

Book: Straight Talk About Psychiatric Medications for Kids by Timothy E. Wilens (Available at Amazon)

American Academy of Pediatrics: www.healthychildren.org/English/health-issues/conditions/adhd/pages/Determining-ADHD-Medication-Treatments.aspx

American Academy of Child Adolescent Psychiatry: www.aacap.org/AACAP/Families_and_Youth/Facts_for_Families/FFF-Guide/Psychiatric-Medication-For-Children-And-Adolescents-Part-I-How-Medications-Are-Used-021.aspx

Children and Adults with Attention-Deficit/Hyperactivity Disorder (CHADD): https://chadd.org/for-parents/managing-medication/

Oppositional Defiant Disorder

- ODD Factsheet: https://kidshealth.org/en/parents/odd-factsheet.html#catfactsheet
- ODD: https://www.mayoclinic.org/diseases-conditions/oppositional-defiant-disorder/symptoms-causes/syc-20375831
- ODD: https://www.hopkinsmedicine.org/health/conditions-and-diseases/oppositional-defiant-disorder

Autism

- National Institute of Mental Health: www.nimh.nih.gov/health/topics/autism-spectrum-disorders-asd
- Autism Speaks: www.autismspeaks.org/what-autism
- Cleveland Clinic: https://my.clevelandclinic.org/health/diseases/8855-autism

Speech Language Therapy

- American Speech-Language-Hearing Association: www.asha.org
- I Can (helps children communicate): www.ican.org.uk

Gifted Children

- National Association for Able Children in Education: www.nace.co.uk

General

- A full database of psychologists, clinical and other, self-employed or employed, may be found at: www.bps.org.uk
- Specialist teachers recommend the Student Organiser Pack which may be obtained from the Communications And Learning Skills Centre: www.calsc.co.uk
- OCD Action: www.ocdaction.org.uk
- The website of the Selective Mutism group (SMG-CAN) may be found at www.selectivemutism.org and offers membership for affected families and, therefore, the resources of a network, mutual support and strategic information.
- Resources for social and personal development: www.incentiveplus.co.uk/

Notes

1. www.readingrockets.org/article/dyslexia-schools-assessment-and-identification.
2. NOTE: This is not an exhaustive list of tests and for further information regarding more tests, you can visit the following websites:
   - www.sess.ie/dyslexia-section/lists-tests. www.understood.org/articles/en/tests-for-dyslexia Retrieved July 21, 2021.
   - www.readingrockets.org/article/dyslexia-schools-assessment-and-identification.
   - www.understood.org/articles/en/rapid-automatized-naming-tests-what-you-need-to-know
3. **Bramley, W**. *Units Of Sound*. Cambridge: LDA, with the Dyslexia Institute, 1998.
4. *Toe By Toe*, a phonics-based system of reading tuition which seeks to establish a basis of good decoding skills, is obtainable from its author, **Keda Cowling**, at 8 Green Road, Baildon, West Yorkshire BD17 5HL; phone 01274 598807.

References

Becker, N., Vasconcelos, M., Oliveira, V., Dos Santos, F., Bizarro, L., De Almeida, R., De Salles, J., & Carvalho, M. (2017). Genetic and environmental risk factors for developmental dyslexia in children: Systematic review of the last decade. *Developmental Neuropsychology*, *42*(7–8), 423–445.

Bell, S. (2013). Professional development for specialist teachers and assessors of students with literacy difficulties/dyslexia: 'To learn how to assess and support children with dyslexia'. *Journal of Research in Special Educational Needs*, *13*(1), 104–113.

Berninger, V. W. (2007). *Process assessment of the learner-II*. Harcourt Assessment.

Ehri, L. C. (1995). Phases of development in learning to read words by sight. *Journal of Research in Reading*, *18*(2), 116–125.

Ehri, L. C., & McCormick, S. (1998). Phases of word learning: Implications for instruction with delayed and disabled readers. *Reading & Writing Quarterly: Overcoming Learning Difficulties*, *14*(2), 135–163.

Einarsdottir, E., Peyrard-Janvid, M., Darki, F., Tuulari, J., Merissari, H., Karlsson, L., Scheinin, N., Saunavaara, J., Parkkola, R., Kantojavri, K., Ammala, A., Yu, N., Matsson, H., Nopola-Hemmi, J., Karlsson, H., Paunio, T., Klingberg, T., Leinonen, E., & Kere, J. (2017). Identification of NCAN as a candidate gene for developmental dyslexia. *Scientific Reports*, *7*, 9294.

Everatt, J., Smythe, I., Adams, E., & Ocampo, D. (2000). Dyslexia screening measures and bilingualism. *Dyslexia: An International Journal of Research and Practice*, *6*, 42–56. John Wiley & Sons.

Fuchs, D., Compton, D. L., Fuchs, L. S., & Bryant, J. (2008). Making "secondary intervention" work in a three-tier responsiveness-to-intervention model: Findings from the first-grade longitudinal reading study at the national research center on learning disabilities. *Reading and Writing: An Interdisciplinary Journal*, *21*, 413–436.

Fuchs, D., & Fuchs, L. S. (2005). Responsiveness-to-intervention: A blueprint for practitioners, policymakers, and parents. *Teaching Exceptional Children*, *38*, 57–61.

Fuchs, L. S., & Stecker, P. M. (2003). *Scientifically based progress monitoring*. National Center on Student Progress Monitoring. Retrieved May 15, 2009.

Galaburda, A. (1989). Ordinary and extraordinary brain development: Anatomical variation in developmental dyslexia. *Annals of Dyslexia*, *39*, 65–80.

Giovagnoli, S., Mandolesi, L., Magri, S., Gualtieri, L., Fabbri, D., Tossani E., & Benassi, M. (2020). Internalizing symptoms in developmental dyslexia: A comparison between primary and secondary school. *Frontiers in Psychology*, *11*, 461.

Gough, P. B., & Tunmer, W. E. (1986). Decoding, reading, and reading disability. *Remedial and Special Education*, *7*(1), 6–10. https://doi.org/10.1177/074193258600700104

References

Hou, F., Qi, L., Liu, L., Luo, X., Gu, H., Xie, X., Li, X., Zhang, J., & Song, R. (2018). Validity and reliability of the dyslexia checklist for Chinese children. *Frontiers in Psychology, 9*, 1915–1915.

Hudson Kam, C. L., & Newport, E. L. (2005). Regularizing unpredictable variation: The roles of adult and child learners in language formation and change. *Language Learning and Development, 1*(2), 151–195.

Kilpatrick, D. A. (2015). *Essentials of assessing, preventing, and overcoming reading difficulties. Essay*. John Wiley & Sons.

Kirby, P., Nation, K., Snowling, M., & Whyte, W. (2020). The problem of dyslexia: Historical perspectives. *Oxford Review of Education, 46*(4), 409–413. doi:10.1080/03054985.2020.1770020

Lindstrom, J. (2019). Dyslexia in the schools: Assessment and identification. *Teaching Exceptional Children, 51*(3), 189–200. Sage Publications.

Livingston, E., Siegel, L., & Ribary, U. (2018). Developmental dyslexia: Emotional impact and consequences. *Australian Journal of Learning Difficulties, 23*(2), 107–135.

Lovett, M., et al. (2017). Early intervention for children at risk for reading disabilities: The impact of grade at intervention and individual differences on intervention outcomes. *Journal of Educational Psychology © 2017 American Psychological Association, 109*(7), 889–914.

Mather, N., & Wendling, B. (2012). *Essentials of dyslexia assessment and intervention* (Essentials of Psychological Assessment Series). John Wiley & Sons Inc.

McMaster, K. L., & Wagner, D. (2007). Monitoring response to general education instruction. In S. R. Jimerson, M. K. Burns, & A. M. VanDerHeyden (Eds.), *Handbook of response to intervention: The science and practice of assessment and intervention* (pp. 223–233). Springer.

Reid, G., & Guise, J. (2017). *The dyslexia assessment*. Bloomsbury Publishing.

Reid, G., & Guise, J. (2019). *Assessment for dyslexia: A concise guide for teachers and parents*. Jessica Kingsley.

Reilly, D., Neumann, D. L., & Andrews, G. (2019). Gender differences in reading and writing achievement: Evidence from the National Assessment of Educational Progress (NAEP). *American Psychologist, 74*(4), 445–458. https://doi.org/10.1037/amp0000356

Singleton, C., Horne, J., & Simmons, F. (2009). Computerized screening for dyslexia in adults. *Journal of Research in Reading, 32*(1), 137–152.

Slavin, R. E., & Madden, N. A. (2006). Reducing the gap: Success for all and the achievement of African American students. *The Journal of Negro Education, 75*(3), 389–400. www.jstor.org/stable/40026810

Snowling, M. J. (2013). Early identification and interventions for dyslexia: A contemporary view. *Journal of Research in Special Educational Needs, 13*, 7–14.

Stahl, S. A., & Kuhn, M. R. (2002). Making it sound like language: Developing fluency (Center for the Improvement of Early Reading Achievement). *The Reading Teacher, 55*(6), 582–585.

Torgesen, J., Morgan, S., & Davis, C. (1992). Effects of two types of phonological awareness training on word learning in kindergarten children. *Journal of Educational psychology, 84*(3), 364.

Torgesen, J., Wagner, R., Rashotte, C, Burgess, S., & Hecht, S. (1997). Contributions of phonological awareness and rapid automatic naming ability to the growth of word-reading skills in second-to fifth-grade children. *Scientific Studies of Reading, 1*(2), 161–185.

U.S. Department of Health and Human Services. (n.d.). Report of the National Reading Panel: Teaching Children to read: Reports of the subgroups. Eunice Kennedy Shriver National Institute of Child Health and Human Development. https://www.nichd.nih.gov/publications/product/247

Vaughn, S., Linan-Thompson, S., & Hickman, P. (2003). Response to instruction as a means of identifying students with reading/learning disabilities. *Exceptional Children, 69*, 391–409.

Wagner, R., Zirps, F., Edwards, A., Wood, S., Joyner, R., Becker, B., Lie, G., & Beal, B. (2020). The prevalence of dyslexia: A new approach to its estimation. *Journal of Learning Disabilities, 53*(5).

Index

accelerated 19, 60
access 2, 7, 14, 23, 61, 73
accommodations 5, 9, 11, 14, 19, 42, 47, 55, 59–60, 63
accredited 76
accuracy 7, 22, 32–33, 49–50, 53–54, 57, 70–71
Achenbach 38, 74
achievement vi, 42, 45, 49, 70–73, 82
acquisition 21, 25, 37, 55–56
ADD 74–75
ADDISS 79
ADHD 9, 14–15, 22, 25–26, 38, 41, 44–45, 50–51, 53, 61, 63–65, 74–75, 79
administer 7–8, 34, 39, 60
adolescent 75, 79
adults 11, 15, 22, 60, 64–65, 75, 76, 82
affect 3, 14, 18, 22, 36, 48, 50, 52, 62, 69
anxiety 5, 13–15, 18, 22, 26, 38, 40–41, 51, 54, 58, 61, 64–65, 75
arithmetic 21, 24–25, 37
ascertain 8, 13, 15, 17–18, 26, 34, 39, 42, 47–48, 60
ASD 9, 51
assessment v–vi, viii–12, 22, 27–40, 47, 51, 59–60, 70–75, 81–82
assistive 14, 60–63
asthma 24
attain 3, 28, 40
attention 4, 6, 9, 12–13, 16, 18, 22, 24, 35, 38, 41, 44, 49–50, 52–54, 58, 63–65
atypical 13, 22, 38, 42, 50–51, 64
autism 9, 13, 23, 38, 51, 80
awareness vii, 3, 6, 18, 27–29, 49–50, 53–54, 56–58, 72–73, 82

Baddely 73
Bangor 31
Barton 77
BASC 38, 42, 51, 74

Becker, N. 1, 81, 83
behaviour 4, 6, 9, 12–13, 15, 20, 22–26, 35, 37–38, 40–42, 48, 50–51, 63–65, 68, 79
Belfield 32
Berlin, R. vii, 1
Berninger, V.W. 72, 81
Binet 37
birth 11, 23–24, 26, 69
blending 27–28, 35, 49
Bloomsbury 36, 82
Bramley, W. 76, 80
BrightStart 31, 76
Bryant, J. 73, 81
Burgess, S. 82
Burns, M.K. 82
Bury 32

caregivers 6, 20
categories 13–14, 33, 77
CBM 31, 34–35
CBT 15
CCEA 32
CHADD 79
checklist 28, 33, 82
chunking 59
Claro 78
cloze 17, 40, 72
clumsy 29–30
coexisting 1, 3–4, 20, 22, 25, 34, 39, 50–52, 55, 63
cognitive 3, 6, 8–10, 15–16, 27, 37, 39, 48, 53, 74–75
communication 4, 16, 28, 40, 51, 78
comorbidities 1, 16
competence 22, 62
compliance 25–26, 50, 63–64
composite 31, 44–46
conditions 4, 14–16, 20, 22, 25, 34, 39–40, 50, 52, 55, 63, 65–66, 79

crested 75
Crossbow Education 76
CTOPP 53, 74

DAS 37
Davis, C. 82
deficits 1, 21, 35, 46, 53-55, 76
depression 5, 13, 15, 22, 26, 38, 51, 64-65, 75
diagnosed vii-viii, 4-5, 11-12, 20, 22-25, 44, 50-51, 55-56, 60-63
diagnosing 16
diagnosis 1-2, 5, 7-11, 17-18, 28, 38-39, 42, 45, 47-48, 50-51, 54
DIBELS 31, 60
disorder 1, 3, 9, 12, 15-16, 18, 22-23, 38, 40, 42, 48, 50-55, 64, 79-80
DSM 2, 53
dyspraxia 79

EarlyBird 31, 60, 76
Earobics 78
easyCBM 31
Edwards, A. 83
effective 2-3, 8, 10, 20, 35, 56-60, 64-65
efficient 10, 61, 63
Ehri, L.C. 27-28, 71, 81
Elbeheri, G. i, iii-iv, viii
elements 1-2, 6, 10, 17, 32, 37, 39, 49, 56
eligibility 5-6, 8-11, 17, 38-39, 42
Ellis, T. 77
emotional 4, 9, 12-15, 19-20, 22, 37, 40-42, 48, 50-51, 63-64, 74
enables viii, 2, 5, 77
encoding 72
encopresis 23, 65
enuresis 23, 65
evaluate 3, 14, 28, 33, 37, 39, 49, 51, 59, 62
evaluation viii, 2, 7-9, 17-18, 24, 34, 37-42, 47-49, 52-53, 72, 79
Everatt, J. 8, 81
evidence 4, 7, 19, 34, 47, 55, 57, 60, 63, 70, 74
excessive 12, 36, 53-54, 58
executive 9, 13, 22, 25, 39, 50, 74-75
EYES 32

facilitate vii, 11, 16-17, 27, 33, 63
factor 14, 40, 44, 51, 53, 58
factsheet 75, 79
FastBridge 31
FastForWord 78

Fawcett 31
feedback 15, 34, 59
fluency 32-33, 53, 70-72, 78
fluid 44-45, 52
focus 2, 9, 11, 13-14, 16, 19, 23-25, 32, 37, 39, 47, 49, 51, 55, 57, 64
formulation vi, 47-54, 58, 63
Frederickson 73
Fuchs, D. 34-35, 81
functions 2, 6, 8-9, 12-13, 17-18, 22, 25, 37-39, 47-50, 59

Galaburda, A. 1, 81
Gathercool 73
genetic 1, 14
genre 7, 49-50
Gillingham 75-77
Giovagnoli, S. 5, 81
given vii, 4, 20, 52, 55, 58, 60, 63
Gough, P.B. 32, 56, 81
grade 3, 14, 16, 25-28, 33, 44, 54, 57, 59-60, 67, 70, 76, 78, 81-82
grapheme 57
Gray 72
growth 3, 34, 55, 82
Guise, J. 5, 28, 36, 82

handwriting 4, 30, 61
Harcourt 31, 81
Hasborouck 33
Hickman, P. 83
Hodder 32, 71-73
homework 25, 30, 62-64, 68
Houghton 31
Houston 28
Hudson Kam, C.L. 33, 71, 82
Hulme 73
hyperactivity 9, 18, 22, 38, 41, 50, 53-54

iansyst 79
ican 80
ICD 2, 53-54
IDA i, 2-3, 32, 39, 48, 55, 75-76
identification iv, 7-8, 21, 25, 35, 48-49, 71, 80, 82
idiomatic 51, 77
idiosyncratic 29
illnesses 23-24, 52, 69
impact vii, 1-4, 6-7, 9-10, 12-15, 18, 22-26, 37, 40, 43, 48-54, 56, 61, 63, 65, 69, 82
impairment 12-14, 16-17, 20, 41, 47-48, 50-51, 63, 74-75
impulsivity 22, 41, 50, 63

IMSLEC 76
inattention 22, 40, 50, 53–54
indicator 8, 21, 26, 43
inhibitors 65
instructions 29–30, 34, 36, 67
instruments 6–8, 10, 15, 17, 27–28, 32, 34–35, 37–39, 49–51, 60, 74
intellectual 41, 48
intensity 14, 55, 60
interventions 8, 14–16, 19, 34–35, 42, 47, 55, 57–58, 60, 64, 82
IRIS 32–33, 70

Kurzweil 78

Lastinger 28, 60
LEFT v, viii, 12–19, 37, 39
Linan-Thompson, S. 83
Lindstrom, J. 11, 82
LiPS 77
Livingston, E. 5, 82
Lovett, M. 7, 57, 82

Macmillan 71, 73
Madden, N.A. 35, 82
McCormick, S. 71, 81
Miles 31
modification 14–15, 63–65
morphology 56
Murray 32
mutism 80

NAEP 3, 32, 82
neurodevelopmental 9, 15, 24, 39
NFER-Nelson 32
NJCLD i
nonwords 71
norms 70

OCD 80
ODD 15
onset 6, 27, 35
orthographic 45–46
ortonacademy 75

paediatrics 66
Peabody Picture Vocabulary Test (PPVT) 34
percentile 43–46
perceptual 9, 37
phonemic 56, 71
pragmatic 23, 26, 51

preferential 15, 63–64
psychoeducational 9, 37–38

Quickscan 31

Reid, G. 5, 28, 36, 73, 82
remediation i, 9–11, 16, 19, 25, 27, 32–33, 42, 55, 57–60
reuptake 65
rhyming 4, 21, 28, 44, 56, 66
RTI vi, 7–8, 14, 34–35, 60, 70

SCARED 42, 54, 75
screener 28, 31
screening tools, 8, 30–32, 69–70, 75–76
segmentation 27, 35
semantics 49, 56
Slingerland 32
Snowling, M.J. 7, 73, 82
Sonday 76
Springer 82
SSRI 65
standardized 9, 12, 34, 47, 70
Stanford 37
stimulant 64
Stoughton 32, 71–73
studyscan 31
support vii–viii, 2, 7–8, 11, 17, 27, 63, 79, 80–81
systematic 59, 81

THRASS 76
Torgesen, J. 73, 82
TOWRE 49, 71
Tridas, Eric Q. i, iii–iv, viii
Tunmer, W.E. 32, 56, 81
Turner, M. 69

Vanderbilt 36, 70
Vaughn, S. 35, 83

Wagner, R. 3, 35, 82–83
Wechsler 70–73
Weedon 73
Wendling, B. 6, 56, 82
WHO 2
Wiley, J. 81–82
Wilson 76
WISC 37, 44, 46, 49, 52–53
Woodcock 37, 49, 70–73
writing 77, 81

Printed in Great Britain
by Amazon